The Law of
Attraction

Other Hay House Titles by Esther and Jerry Hicks

(The Teachings of Abraham)

Books, Calendar, and Card Decks

The Amazing Power of Deliberate Intent
(also available in Spanish)

Ask and It Is Given (also available in Spanish)

Ask and It Is Given Cards

Ask and It Is Given Perpetual Flip Calendar (available July 2007)

The Astonishing Power of Emotions (available September 2007)

The Law of Attraction Cards (coming in 2008)

Manifest Your Desires (available June 2008)

Sara, Book 1: Sara Learns the Secret about the <u>Law of Attraction</u>

Sara, Book 2: Solomon's Fine Featherless Friends
(available October 2007)

Sara, Book 3: A Talking Owl Is Worth a Thousand Words!
(available April 2008)

The Teachings of Abraham Well-Being Cards

CD Programs

The Amazing Power of Deliberate Intent
(Parts I and II: two 4-CD sets)

Ask and It Is Given (Parts I and II: two 4-CD sets)

The Astonishing Power of Emotions
(Parts I and II: two 4-CD sets) (available September 2007)

The Law of Attraction (5-CD set)

The Law of Attraction in Action (2-CD set)

-:[🕮]:-

Please visit Hay House USA: **www.hayhouse.com**®
Hay House Australia: **www.hayhouse.com.au**
Hay House UK: **www.hayhouse.co.uk**
Hay House South Africa: **orders@psdprom.co.za**
Hay House India: **www.hayhouseindia.co.in**

To: Octavio,
I give and dedicate this book to you with joy, happiness and Love ♡ ∽ María

The Law of
Attraction

The Basics of the Teachings of Abraham

ESTHER AND JERRY HICKS
(The Teachings of Abraham™)

2006

HAY HOUSE, INC.
Carlsbad, California
London • Sydney • Johannesburg
Vancouver • Hong Kong • New Delhi

Published and distributed in the United States by: Hay House, Inc.: www.hayhouse. com • *Published and distributed in Australia by:* Hay House Australia Pty. Ltd.: www. hayhouse.com.au • *Published and distributed in the United Kingdom by:* Hay House UK, Ltd.: www.hayhouse.co.uk • *Published and distributed in the Republic of South Africa by:* Hay House SA (Pty), Ltd.: orders@psdprom.co.za • *Distributed in Canada by:* Raincoast: www.raincoast.com • *Published in India by:* Hay House Publishers India: www.hayhouse.co.in

Editorial supervision: Jill Kramer • *Design:* Tricia Breidenthal

The Law of Attraction, The Teachings of Abraham, The Art of Allowing, Segment Intending, and The Science of Deliberate Creation are registered trademarks of Esther and Jerry Hicks.

Library of Congress Cataloging-in-Publication Data

Abraham (Spirit)
  The law of attraction : the basics of the teachings of Abraham / [channelled by] Esther and Jerry Hicks.
    p. cm.
  "The teachings of Abraham."
  ISBN-13: 978-1-4019-1227-7 (tradepaper) • ISBN-13: 978-1-4019-1759-3 (hardcover)
  1. Spirit writings. I. Hicks, Esther. II. Hicks, Jerry. III. Title.
  BF1301.A18 2006
  133.9'3--dc22   2006020009

Hardcover: **ISBN 13:** 978-1-4019-1759-3 • **ISBN 10:** 1-4019-1759-3
Tradepaper: **ISBN 13:** 978-1-4019-1227-7 • **ISBN 10:** 1-4019-1227-3

10 09 08 07   13 12 11 10
1st edition, October 2006
10th edition, March 2007

Printed in the United States of America

—◦[▨]◦—

This book is dedicated to all of you who, in your desire for enlightenment and Well-Being, have asked the questions this book has answered; and to the four delightful children of our children, who are examples of what the book teaches: Laurel (8); Kevin (5); Kate (4); and Luke (1), who are not yet asking because they have not yet forgotten.

And these teachings are especially dedicated to Louise Hay, whose desire to ask and learn—and disseminate around this planet—the principles of Well-Being, has led her to create the Hay House publishing company, which has enabled the distribution of so much joy throughout the world.

—◦[▨]◦—

Contents

PART II: The *Law of Attraction*™

PART IV: The *Art of Allowing*™

PART V: *Segment Intending*™

Foreword

by Neale Donald Walsch, the best-selling author of
The Conversations with God series and
Home with God in a Life That Never Ends

This is it. Here they are. You don't have to go any further. Put all the other books down, un-enroll from all the workshops and seminars, and tell your life coach you won't need to be calling anymore.

Because this is it: everything you need to know about life and how to make it work. Here they are: all the rules of the road for this extraordinary journey. All the tools with which to create the experiences you've always wanted. You don't have to go any further than where you are right now.

Indeed, look at what you've done already.

Just look.

I mean, *right now,* look at what you're holding in your hands.

You did that. You put this book right here, right where it is, right in front of your eyes. You manifested it, out of the clear blue sky. That alone is all the evidence you need that *this book works.*

Do you understand? No, no, don't jump over this. It's important that you really hear this. I'm telling you that you are holding in your hands the best proof you could ever give yourself that the *Law of Attraction* is real, is effective, and produces *physical outcomes in the real world.*

Let me explain.

Somewhere in the deep reaches of your consciousness, somewhere in an important place in your mind, you set an intention to receive this message, or this book would never have found its way to you.

This is no small thing here. This is a big deal. Believe me, it's a big deal. Because *you are about to create exactly what you set your intention to create:* a major change in your life.

That *was* your intention, wasn't it? Of course it was. What is occurring as you read these words wouldn't be happening if you hadn't placed your attention on a deep desire to lift your day-to-day experience to a new level. You've wanted to do this for a long time. Your only questions have been: *How? What are the rules? What are the tools?*

Well, here they are. You asked for them, you got 'em. And that's the very first rule, by the way. What you ask for, you get. But there's more to it than that—lots more. And that's what this extraordinary book is about. Here, you're not only going to be given some pretty amazing tools, but *instructions on how to use them.*

Have you ever wished that life came with an instruction book?

Hey, good wishing. Now it does.

We have Esther and Jerry Hicks to thank for that. And, of course, Abraham. (They will tell you all about who *that* is in the fascinating, exhilarating text to follow.) Esther and Jerry are devoting their lives to the joy of sharing the wondrous messages that Abraham has given them. I admire and love them so much for this; and I am so, so grateful, for they are truly extraordinary people on a glorious mission to bring glory to the mission upon which we have *all* embarked: the living and the experiencing of the glory of Life itself, and of Who We Really Are.

I know that you will be so impressed, and so blessed, by what you find here. I know that reading this book will produce a turning point in your life. Here is not only a description of the most important law of the universe (the only one you'll ever need to know about, really), but an easy-to-understand explanation of the *mechanics of life.* This is breathtaking information. This is monumental data. This is brilliant, flashing insight.

There are very few books about which I would say what I am going to say next. *Read every word here, and do everything this book says.* It answers all the questions you have so earnestly asked in your heart. So—may I be this direct?—pay attention.

This book is about *how* to pay attention, and if you pay attention to *how* to pay attention, your every intention can be made manifest in your reality—and that will change your life forever.

Preface

by Jerry Hicks

T he groundbreaking philosophy of practical spirituality that you are about to discover in this book was first revealed to Esther and me in 1986, in response to the very long list of questions that I had been without answer for, for many years.

Within these pages you'll find the basics of the *Teachings of Abraham*™ as they were lovingly spoken to us in the very first days of our interactions with them (please note that the singular name "Abraham" is a *group* of loving entities, which is why they're referred to in the plural).

The recordings from which this book evolved were first formally published in 1988 as part of an album of ten *Special Subjects* cassette recordings. But since that time, many aspects of Abraham's basic teachings regarding the *Universal Law of Attraction* have been published in varied forms of books, CDs, DVDs, card decks, calendars, articles, radio and television shows, and workshops, as well as by the many other best-selling authors who have incorporated the teachings of Abraham into their teachings. However, never before this book, *The Law of Attraction,* have these original teachings been published in their entirety in a single volume.

(Should you like to hear one of the original recordings from the series, you can find our free *Introduction to Abraham* as a 70-minute download at our Website: **www.abraham-hicks.com**.)

This book was created by transcribing our original *"Abraham Basics" Starter Set* of five CDs and then asking Abraham to edit them slightly to enhance the readability of the spoken word. Abraham has also added several new passages for the sake of clarity and continuity.

Millions of readers, listeners, and viewers have been enjoying the value they've received from these teachings. And Esther and I are thrilled to offer to you, in this *Law of Attraction* format, the original basic teachings of Abraham.

But how does this book compare to Abraham's *Ask and It Is Given?* Well, consider *The Law of Attraction* the basic primer from which all of the other teachings have flowed. And consider *Ask and It Is Given* to be the most comprehensive volume of the first 20 years of Abraham's teachings.

Revisiting this life-changing material in the preparation of the publication of this book has been a wonderful experience for Esther and me, for we've been reminded of these basic and simple *Laws* that Abraham effectively explained to us so many years ago.

Since originally receiving this material, Esther and I have done our best to apply to our own lives what we have learned about these *Laws*, and the marvelous progression of our joyous lives is astounding. We took Abraham at their word because everything they told us made so much sense to us, but the application of these teachings has now been proven in our day-to-day experience. And it is with extraordinary joy that we can tell you—from our own personal experience: *This works!*

ঔ ঔ ঔ   ৡ ৡ ৡ

(**Editor's Note:** Please note that since there aren't always physical English words to perfectly express the Non-Physical thoughts that Esther receives, she sometimes forms new combinations of words, as well as using standard words in new ways—for example, capitalizing or italicizing them when normally they wouldn't be—in order to express new ways of looking at life.)

PART I

Our Path to the Abraham Experience

INTRODUCTION

by Jerry Hicks

W e've written this book to introduce you to *Universal Laws* and practical processes that will guide you clearly and precisely to the realization of your natural state of Well-Being. Your reading of this book will give you the unique and beneficial experience of hearing precise, powerful answers to questions that I've accumulated from a lifetime of asking. And your successful utilization of this joy-based philosophy of practical spirituality will also help you guide others to living whatever they would consider to be the perfect life.

Many have indicated to me that my questions, in many ways, have mirrored their own. And so, as you experience the clarity and brilliance of Abraham's answers, not only will you likely begin to feel a true satisfaction that long-asked questions have been answered, but you'll discover, as we (Esther and I) have, a renewed enthusiasm for your own life experience. And as you, from your fresh new outlook on life, begin to apply the practical processes that are offered here, you'll discover that you can deliberately create for yourself anything that you want to do, be, or have.

It seems to me that my life, from as far back as I can remember, produced a stream of seemingly never-ending questions to which I wasn't able to find satisfactory answers, for I had strongly wanted to discover a philosophy of life that was based on absolute truth. But once Abraham came into our experience—revealing to Esther and me their explanation of the powerful *Laws* of the Universe, coupled with effective processes that helped us to turn ideology and theory into practical results—I came to realize that the steady stream of books, teachers, and life experiences that I *did* encounter on my path were the perfect steps along the way to the discovery of Abraham.

I like thinking about the opportunity that you now have as you read this book to discover for yourself the value of what Abraham offers, because I know how these teachings have enhanced our life experience. I'm also aware that you would not now be holding this book in your hands if your life experience had not prepared you (as my life has prepared me) for receiving this information.

I feel an eagerness for you to dive into this book to discover the simple and powerful *Laws* and practical processes that Abraham offers so that you may begin to *deliberately* attract into *your* experience everything that *you* desire, and so that you may release anything from your experience that you don't want.

A Steady Stream of Religious Groups

My parents weren't religious people, so I don't really understand why it was that I felt such a powerful compulsion to find a church and become involved in the tenets of its religion, but it was a powerful force within me as I was growing up. Maybe it was an attempt to fill the very real void that I felt deep inside, or maybe it was because so many others around me were demonstrating their religious fervor and their certainty that they had discovered *truth*.

During my first 14 years, I lived in 18 homes in six states, so I had the opportunity to evaluate a wide variety of philosophies. In any case, I systematically marched myself into church after church, each time hoping with all my heart that inside *these* doors I would find what I was looking for. But as I moved from one religious or philosophical group to another, my disappointment grew as they each exclaimed *their* rightness, at the same time declaring all of the others *wrong*. And in this environment, with my heart sinking again and again, I knew that I hadn't found the answers I was looking for. (It was only after discovering the teachings of Abraham that I've been able to come to understand, and to no longer feel negative emotion about, those apparent philosophical contradictions.) And so, my search for answers continued.

A Ouija Board Spells the Alphabet

Even though I'd never had any personal experience with a Ouija board, I did, nevertheless, have strong negative opinions about it. I believed that it was, at best, only a game, and at worst, an absolute hoax. So in 1959 when friends in Spokane, Washington, presented me with the idea of playing with the board, I immediately dismissed it as ridiculous. But as my friends persisted, and subsequently presented me with my first actual experience with it, I saw for myself that a real phenomenon was occurring.

Therefore, since I was still searching for answers to my lifelong list of questions, I asked the board, "How can I become truly good?" At first, and with dramatic speed, it spelled the alphabet, and then the planchette pointed to **R-E-A-D**.

"Read what?" I asked. It spelled **B-O-O-K-S**. And then when I asked, "What books?" it spelled (again with that first dramatic speed): **A N Y A N D A L L B Y A L B E R T S C H W E I T Z E R**. My friends had not heard of Albert Schweitzer, and while I knew very little about him, my curiosity was piqued, to say the least, and I decided to do some research to find out about this man who had just come into my conscious awareness in this truly extraordinary way.

In the first library I could find, I discovered a very large selection of books written by Albert Schweitzer, and I systematically read them all. And while I cannot say that I discovered any specific answers to my long list of questions, Schweitzer's book *The Quest of the Historical Jesus* especially opened my mind to the awareness that there are many more ways of looking at things than I had been willing to consider.

My enthusiasm for what I had hoped was to be a window into powerful enlightenment and answers to all of my questions was eventually dashed as I found neither powerful enlightenment from the Ouija board nor answers to all of my questions, but it had certainly awakened within me the realization that there was an avenue of intelligent communication available that I had never believed was possible before I had experienced it myself.

The Ouija board wouldn't work for me at all when I used it on my own, but I tried it on hundreds of people in my travels as an entertainer, and I found three people who had success with it. With some friends in Portland, Oregon (whom the board *did* work for), we "talked" for hundreds of hours with what we thought to be Non-Physical Beings. What an entertaining parade of pirates, priests, politicians, and rabbis conversed with us! It was much like the kind of fascinating conversations you might engage in at parties, with individuals offering a wide variety of agendas, attitudes, and intellects.

I have to say that I learned nothing of value from that board that I could use in my own life—or that I wanted to teach anybody else—so one day I just threw it away, and that was the end of that stage of my interest or activity with the Ouija board. However, this remarkable experience—especially with the Intelligence that encouraged my reading of books—not only awakened within me an understanding that there is much more "out there" than I currently understood, but it provoked within me an even more powerful desire to find answers. I came to believe that it was possible to tap into an Intelligence that had practical answers to questions about how the Universe works, why we are all here, how we can live more joyous lives, and how we can fulfill our reasons for being here.

Think and Grow Rich

Perhaps the first experience of actually finding practical answers to my growing list of questions came to me in the discovery of a fascinating book while I was doing concerts in a series of colleges and universities in 1965. The book was lying on a coffee table in the lobby of a small motel somewhere in Montana, and I remember a contradiction formulating within me as I held it and looked at the words on the front cover: *Think and Grow Rich!* by Napoleon Hill.

This title was off-putting to me, for I, like so many others, had been taught to shore up my negative impression of rich people as justification for my own lack of easily acquired resources. There was something undeniably compelling about this book, though, and after I'd gotten only about 12 pages into it, the hair was standing up all over my body, and thrill bumps were rippling up and down my spine.

We've now come to understand that these physical, visceral sensations are confirming evidence that we're currently on the path to something of extreme value, but even then I felt that this book awakened within me the knowledge that my thoughts are important, and that my life experience somehow reflects the contents of my thoughts. The book was compelling and interesting, and it inspired a desire within me to attempt to follow the suggestions that were offered—and I did.

Utilizing the teachings worked so well for me, in fact, that in a very brief amount of time I was able to build a multinational business, giving me the opportunity to touch the lives of thousands of people in a meaningful way. I even began teaching the principles that I was learning. But although I had personally received incredible value from Napoleon Hill's life-changing book, many of the lives of those I was teaching weren't as dramatically improved as mine had been no matter how many courses they took, so my search for more specific answers continued.

Seth Speaks about Creating Your Reality

While my lifelong quest to discover meaningful answers to my questions still persisted, and my desire to find a way to help others more effectively achieve their goals loomed larger than ever before, I was temporarily distracted from all of that by the new life that Esther and I were making together in Phoenix, Arizona. We were married in 1980 after knowing each other for a few years, and we found ourselves to be inexplicably compatible. We were experiencing joy, day after wonderful day, exploring our new city, making our new home, and discovering our new life together. And while Esther didn't exactly share my thirst for knowledge or my hunger for answers, she was eager about life, always happy, and very nice to be with.

One day while passing time in a library, I spotted a book entitled *Seth Speaks* by Jane Roberts, and it seemed that before I could extract the book from the shelf, I felt my hairs standing on end again, and my body was again covered in thrill bumps. I leafed through the pages of this book, wondering what it could possibly contain that could be responsible for my emotional response.

During the time that Esther and I had been together, I had discovered only one point of contention between us: She didn't want to hear about my Ouija-board experiences. Whenever I would launch into (what I considered to be) an extremely entertaining account, Esther would leave the room. She'd been taught during her childhood to have tremendous fear of anything that wasn't physical, and since I didn't want to disturb her, I stopped telling those stories, at least while she was around. And so, it wasn't really a surprise to me that Esther didn't want to hear about the book *Seth Speaks* either. . . .

Author Jane Roberts would go into a sort of trance and allow Seth, a Non-Physical personality, to speak through her in order to dictate the series of highly influential *Seth* books. I found the works to be stimulating and fascinating, and I began to see an avenue to some of the answers to my long list of questions. But Esther was frightened by the book. Her discomfort surfaced immediately upon hearing of the manner in which the book had been written, and was powerfully compounded when she viewed the strange-looking picture on the back of the book of Jane, in trance, speaking for Seth.

"You can read the book if you want to," Esther told me, "but please don't bring it into our bedroom."

I've always believed in judging the tree by its fruits, so everything that I consider, I do from the standpoint of how *I* feel about it . . . and there was so much of the Seth material that just felt right to me. So it didn't make any difference to me *where* it came from or *how* it was presented. In essence, I felt that I had found valuable information that *I* could use—and that I could pass on to other people whom I believed could use it. I was excited!

--•⟨ ⬛ ⟩•--

My Fears Were Resolved

by Esther Hicks

I thought it was both very wise and very kind of Jerry not to push the *Seth* books at me, because I really did feel a strong aversion to them. The whole idea of a person being in contact with a Non-Physical Being made me extremely uncomfortable, so, since Jerry didn't want to disturb me, he would get up early in the morning, and while I was still sleeping, he'd read those books to himself. Gradually, when he'd find something that was particularly interesting to him, he would gently slip it into the conversation, and in my less resistant state, I could often hear the value of the idea. Bit by bit, Jerry introduced another concept and another, until I began to feel true interest in those amazing works. Eventually, it became our morning ritual. We would sit together, and Jerry would read to me from the *Seth* books.

My fears weren't grounded in any negative personal experience, but from hearsay that I'd picked up, probably from others who had also picked it up from hearsay. Looking back, it now seems utterly illogical that I had those fears. In any event, I experienced a real change in attitude once I realized that as far as my personal experience was concerned . . . it all felt good.

As time passed, and as my fear of Jane's process in the receiving of the information from Seth subsided, I began to feel immense appreciation for these wonderful books. In fact, we were so happily involved in what we were reading that we thought we would take a trip to New York to meet Jane and her husband, Robert—and even Seth! How far I had come, in that now I actually wanted to meet this Non-Physical Being. But the authors' phone number was unpublished, so we didn't know exactly what to do next to accomplish this meeting.

One day we were eating lunch in a little café next to a bookstore in Scottsdale, Arizona, and Jerry was leafing through a new book he'd just purchased, when a stranger who was sitting nearby asked us, "Have you read any of the *Seth* books?"

We could hardly believe what we were hearing, because we hadn't told a single person that we were reading those books. Then the man asked, "Did you know that Jane Roberts is dead?"

I remember my eyes filling with tears as the impact of these words washed over me. It was as if someone had told me my sister was dead and I hadn't known about it. It was shocking. We felt such disappointment, as we realized that now there would be no possible way for us to meet Jane and Rob . . . or Seth.

Sheila "Channels" Theo

Within a day or so of our hearing about Jane's death, our friends and business associates, Nancy and her husband, Wes, met us for dinner. "We have a tape we want you to hear," Nancy said, pushing a cassette into my hand. Our friends' behavior seemed awkward to me; there was just something odd about it. In fact, I felt the same feeling coming from them that I'd felt from Jerry upon his discovery of the *Seth* books. It was as if they had a secret that they wanted to share but were worried about how we'd respond once it *was* shared.

"What is it?" we asked.

"It's channeled," Nancy whispered.

I don't believe that either Jerry or I had ever heard the word *channeled* offered in that context. "What do you mean, 'channeled'?" I asked.

As Nancy and Wes offered their brief and somewhat disjointed explanation, both Jerry and I realized that they were describing the same process by which the *Seth* books had been written. "Her name is Sheila," they continued, "and she speaks for an entity named Theo. She's coming to Phoenix, and you can make an appointment to talk with her if you want to."

We decided to make an appointment, and I can still remember how excited we were. We met in a beautiful (Frank Lloyd Wright–designed) home in Phoenix. It was broad daylight, and to my relief, nothing even remotely spooky happened. Everything was very comfortable and pleasant. As we sat and "visited" with Theo (well, I should say, as *Jerry* visited with Theo—I don't think I said a word during that meeting), I was absolutely amazed!

Jerry had a notebook full of questions, ones he said he'd saved up since he was six years old. He was so excited, asking question after question, sometimes interrupting in the middle of an answer so that he could get one more question in before our time was up. The half hour passed so quickly, and we felt wonderful!

"Can we come back tomorrow?" I asked, because now I was developing a list of questions that *I* wanted to ask Theo.

Should I Meditate?

When we went back the next day, I asked Theo (through Sheila) what we could do to move faster toward our goals. Theo said: *Affirmations,* and then gave me a wonderful one: *I, Esther Hicks, see and draw to me, through Divine Love, those Beings who seek enlightenment through my process. The sharing will elevate us both, now.*

Jerry and I knew about affirmations; we were already using them. And then I asked, "What else?" Theo replied: *Meditate.* Well, I didn't personally know anybody who was meditating, but the whole idea of it just felt strange to me. It wasn't something that I could see myself doing. Jerry said he associated it with people seeing how bad their lives could become—how much pain or poverty they could take—and still exist. In my mind, meditation belonged in the same weird category as walking on hot coals or lying on beds of nails or standing on one foot all day, holding your hand out asking for a donation.

But then I asked Theo, "Well, what do you mean by 'meditate'?"

Theo responded, *For 15 minutes each day, sit in a quiet room, wear comfortable clothing, and focus on your breathing. And as your mind wanders, and it will, just release the thought and focus back on your breathing.* I thought, *Well, that doesn't sound so weird.*

I asked if I should bring our 14-year-old daughter, Tracy, to meet Theo, and the response was: *If it is her asking, but it is not necessary—for you, too, are channels.* I remember how implausible it seemed that something as strange as being a channel—or as significant as being one—could have not been known by us before now. And then the tape recorder clicked off, indicating that, once again, our time was up.

I couldn't believe how fast the time had passed. And so, as I looked down at my list of still-unanswered questions, Stevie, the friend of Sheila's who was operating the tape recorder and taking notes during our conversation with Theo, perhaps noticed my mild frustration, because she asked, "Do you have one last question? Would you like to know the name of *your* spiritual guide?"

That was not a question that would have occurred to me, because I had never heard the term *spiritual guide.* But I liked the sound of such a thing, so I said, "Yes, who is my spiritual guide?"

Theo said: *We are told it will be given to you directly. You will have a clairaudient experience, and you will know.*

We left that beautiful house that day feeling better than we ever remembered. Theo had encouraged us to meditate together. *Because you are compatible, it will be more powerful.* And so, following Theo's suggestions, we went directly home, put on our bathrobes (our most comfortable clothing), closed the drapes in the living room, and sat with the intention of meditating (whatever that meant). I remember thinking, *I'm going to meditate every day for 15 minutes, and I'm going to find out the name of my spiritual guide.* It felt odd for Jerry and me to be doing this strange thing together, so we sat in large wingback chairs with an étagère between us so we couldn't see each other.

Something Began "Breathing" Me

Theo's instructions on the process of meditation had been very brief: *For 15 minutes each day, sit in a quiet room, wear comfortable clothing, and focus on your breathing. And as your mind wanders, and it will, just release the thought and focus back on your breathing.*

So we set a timer for 15 minutes, and I settled back into my large comfortable chair and focused on my breathing. I began counting my breaths, in and out. Almost immediately I began to feel a sort of numbness come over me. It was an extremely pleasant sensation. I liked it.

The timer sounded its alarm and startled me. As I regained my awareness of Jerry and the room, I exclaimed, "Let's do it again!" We set the timer for another 15 minutes, and again I felt that wonderful feeling of detachment, or numbness. This time I couldn't feel the chair beneath me. It was as if I were suspended there in the room and nothing else was there.

So we set the timer for another 15 minutes, and again I settled into this new delicious feeling of detachment—and then I felt the incredible sensation of being "breathed." It was as if something powerful and loving was breathing the air into my lungs and then drawing the air back out again. I realize now that this was my first powerful contact with Abraham, but at that time, all I knew was that something more loving than anything I'd ever experienced before was flowing throughout my entire body. Jerry said that as he heard the difference in the sound of my breathing, he had looked around the étagère at me, and it appeared to him that I was in a state of ecstasy.

When the timer sounded and I began to regain my conscious awareness of my surroundings, there was the feeling of an Energy moving through me unlike anything that I'd ever felt before. It was the most extraordinary experience of my lifetime, and my teeth buzzed (not chattered) for several minutes.

What an amazing sequence of events had led to this still rather unbelievable meeting with Abraham: Irrational fears that I had carried with me my entire life, which had no actual basis in my own life experience, had been released, and were replaced with a most loving and personal encounter with *Source Energy*. I'd never read anything that had given me any real understanding of what or who God was, but I knew that what I had experienced must surely be just that.

My Nose Spells the Alphabet

Because of the powerful and emotional experience of our very first attempt, we made a decision to set aside 15 or 20 minutes every day to meditate. And so, for approximately nine months, Jerry and I sat in our wingback chairs, silently breathing and feeling Well-Being. And then, right before Thanksgiving of 1985, during a period of meditation, I experienced something new: My head began moving very gently. It was a very pleasant sensation, in my state of detachment, to feel the sensation of that subtle movement. It was almost a feeling of flying.

I didn't really think anything of it, except that I knew *I* wasn't doing it and that it was an extremely pleasant experience. My head moved like that for two or three days whenever we were meditating, and on the third day or so, I realized that my head wasn't just meaninglessly moving around—I was actually spelling letters with my nose as if it were writing on a chalkboard. I exclaimed in amazement, "Jerry, I'm spelling the alphabet with my nose!"

With the conscious realization that something remarkable was happening, and that someone was offering communication to me, intense waves of thrill bumps began moving all through my body. Never before that moment or since have I experienced the intensity of such wonderfully thrilling sensations rippling through my body. And then they spelled: *I am Abraham. I am your spiritual guide. I love you. I am here to work with you.*

Jerry got his notebook and began recording everything that I was awkwardly translating with my nose. Letter by letter, Abraham began answering Jerry's questions, sometimes for hours at a time. We were so excited to have made contact with Abraham in this way!

Abraham Begins to Type the Alphabet

It was a somewhat slow and awkward means of communication, but Jerry was getting answers to his questions, and the experience was absolutely exhilarating for both of us. So, for about two months, Jerry asked questions, Abraham answered by spelling out words by guiding the movements of my nose, and Jerry wrote everything down. Then one night we were lying in bed, and my hand began to softly thump on Jerry's chest. It surprised me, and I explained to him, "That's not me. It must be them." And then I felt a strong impulse to type.

I went to my typewriter and held my hands over the keyboard, and in the same way that my head had been involuntarily moving to spell out the letters in the air with my nose, my hands began to move across the keyboard of my typewriter. They were moving so rapidly and with such power that it was somewhat alarming to Jerry. He stood by ready to grab my hands if necessary because he didn't want my fingers to be hurt. He said they were moving so fast that he could barely see them. But there was nothing to be alarmed about.

My fingers touched every key, many, many times, before they began spelling the letters of the alphabet, and then they proceeded to write nearly a page of: **i w a n t o t y p e i w a n t t o t y p e i w a n t t o t y p e**, with no capitalization and no spaces between the words. Then my fingers began typing a message, slowly and methodically, asking that I go to the typewriter every day for 15 minutes. And so that's the way we communicated for the next two months.

The Typist Becomes the Speaker

One day we were driving on the freeway in our small Cadillac Seville, and on either side of us was a large 18-wheeler truck and trailer. This section of the freeway didn't seem to be banked properly, and as all three of us began making this sweeping turn at the same time, both trucks seemed to be crossing over into our lane. It appeared to us that we were about to be crushed by these large vehicles. In the midst of that intensity of emotion, Abraham began to speak. I felt my jaw tighten (not so different from the sensation of yawning), and then my mouth began to involuntarily form these words: *Take the next exit.* And we did. We sat by that underpass, and Jerry talked to Abraham for many hours that day. It was very exciting!

Although I grew more comfortable every day as the process of my translation of Abraham evolved, I asked Jerry if we could just let this be our secret, because I was afraid of how others might respond if they found out what was happening to me. In time, however, a handful of close friends began gathering to dialogue with Abraham, and it was about a year later that we decided to open these teachings to the public, as we are still continuing to do.

The evolution of my experience in translating the vibration of Abraham continues every day. Every seminar leaves Jerry and me feeling amazement at their (Abraham's) clarity, wisdom, and love.

One day I laughed so hard at this realization: "I was so afraid of the idea of the Ouija board, and now I *am* one."

The Delicious Abraham Experiences Evolve

We're never able to find adequate words to express what we feel for this work with Abraham. Jerry seems to have always known what he wanted most, and he'd found ways to achieve much of it before meeting Abraham. But what he has said is that Abraham has brought to his understanding an awareness of our purpose here, and an absolute clarity of *how* we're getting or not getting, and with that, the knowledge that we have complete control. There are no bad "breaks," no "unlucky" days, and no need to move with the tides that have been moved by someone else. Also, we are free . . . we are the absolute creators of our experience—and we love it!

Abraham has explained that my husband and I were a perfect combination for presenting these teachings because Jerry's powerful desire to find answers to his questions summoned Abraham to us, and I was able to quiet my mind and release resistance in order to allow the answers to come forth.

It takes very little time for me to allow Abraham to begin speaking through me. From my point of view, I just set forth the intention: *Abraham, I want to clearly speak your words,* and then I focus on my breathing. Within a few seconds, I can feel the clarity, love, and power of Abraham rising within me, and then off we go. . . .

I Have a Conversation with Abraham

by Jerry Hicks

So, this adventure with Abraham, through Esther, continues to excite me, for I've discovered an unending resource for answers to the seemingly unending questions that my own life experience continues to give birth to.

For the first several months after meeting Abraham, Esther and I set aside time in every day to talk with Abraham as I began making my way through my evolving list of questions. In time, as Esther relaxed more into the idea of being someone who could quiet her mind and allow this Infinite Intelligence to flow through her, we began to gradually widen the circle of friends and associates who would gather to discuss the details of their lives with Abraham.

It was very early in our experience when I presented Abraham with my list of burning questions. It's my hope that their answers to *my* early questions may also be satisfying to you. Of course, since that defining moment of plying Abraham with *my* questions, we've met thousands of people who have taken these questions even deeper, and who have added their own important questions to the list, to which Abraham has offered their love and brilliance. But here's where I began with Abraham.

(I have no real way of understanding how it is that Esther is able to allow Abraham to speak through her. From my point of view,

Esther closes her eyes and breathes a few very deep, soft breaths. Her head gently nods for a few moments, and then her eyes open and Abraham addresses me directly, as follows.)

We (Abraham) Describe Ourselves as Teachers

Abraham: Good morning! It is nice to have an opportunity to visit. We extend our appreciation to Esther for allowing this communication, and to you for soliciting it. We have been considering the immense value of this interaction, as it will provide an introduction of that which we are to our physical friends. But even more than a mere introduction of Abraham to your physical world, this book will provide an introduction of the role of the Non-Physical in your physical world, for these worlds are inextricably tied together, you know. There is no way of separating one from the other.

Also, in the writing of this book, we are all fulfilling an agreement that we set forth long before you came into your physical bodies. We, Abraham, agreed that we would remain here focused in the broader, clearer, and therefore more powerful Non-Physical perspective, while you, Jerry and Esther, agreed to go forth into your magnificent physical bodies and into the Leading Edge of thought and creation. And once your life experiences had stimulated within you clear and powerful desire, it was our agreement to rendezvous for the purpose of powerful co-creation.

Jerry, we are eager to answer your long list of questions (so deliberately prepared and honed from the contrast of your life experience), for there is much that we want to convey to our physical friends. We want you to understand the magnificence of your Being, and we want you to understand who-you-really-are and why you have come forth into this physical dimension.

It is always an interesting experience to explain to our physical friends those things that are of a Non-Physical nature, because everything that we offer to you must then be translated through the lens of your physical world. In other words, Esther receives our thoughts, like radio signals, at an unconscious level of her Being, and then translates them into physical words and concepts. It is a perfect blending of the physical and Non-Physical that is occurring here.

As we are able to help you understand the existence of the Non-Physical realm from which we are speaking, we will thereby assist you in understanding more clearly who-you-are. For you are, indeed, an extension of that which we are.

There are many of us here, and we are gathered together because of our current matching intentions and desires. In your physical environment, we are called *Abraham,* and we are known as *Teachers,* meaning those who are currently broader in understanding, who may lead others to that broader understanding. We know that words do not teach, that only life experience teaches, but the combination of life experience coupled with words that define and explain can enhance the experience of learning—and it is in that spirit that we offer these words.

There are *Universal Laws* that affect everything in the Universe—everything that is Non-Physical and everything that is physical. These *Laws* are absolute, they are Eternal, and they are omnipresent (or everywhere). When you have a conscious awareness of these *Laws,* and a working understanding of them, your life experience is tremendously enhanced. In fact, only when you have a conscious working knowledge of these *Laws* are you able to be the Deliberate Creator of your own life experience.

You Have an *Inner Being*

While you certainly are the physical Being that you see here in your physical setting, you are much more than that which you see with your physical eyes. You are actually an extension of Non-Physical *Source Energy.* In other words, that broader, older, wiser Non-Physical you is now also focused into the physical Being that you know as you. We refer to the Non-Physical part of you as your *Inner Being.*

Physical Beings often think of themselves as either dead or alive, and in that line of thinking they sometimes acknowledge that they existed in the Non-Physical realm before coming forth into their physical body, and that, following their physical death, they will return to that Non-Physical realm. But few people actually understand that the Non-Physical part of them remains currently, powerfully, and predominantly focused in the Non-Physical realm while a *part* of that perspective flows into this physical perspective and their *now* physical body.

An understanding of both of these perspectives and their relationship to each other is essential for a true understanding of who-you-are and of how to understand what you have intended as you came forth into this physical body. Some call that Non-Physical part the "Higher Self" or "Soul." It matters not what you call it, but it is of great value for you to acknowledge that your *Inner Being* exists, for only when you consciously understand the relationship between you and your *Inner Being* do you have true guidance.

We Do Not Want to Alter Your Beliefs

We come forth not to alter your beliefs, but to reacquaint you with the *Eternal Laws of the Universe* so that you may *intentionally* be the creator that you have come forth to be, for there is not another who attracts into your experience that which you are getting—you are doing it all.

We come forth not to get you to believe anything, for there is nothing that you believe that we do not want you to believe. And as we are viewing this wondrous physical Earth plane, we see great diversity in that which you believe—and in all of that diversity, there is perfect balance.

We will present these *Universal Laws* to you in a simple format. And we will also offer practical processes whereby you may deliberately access the *Laws* for the achievement of whatever is important to you. And although we know that you will revel in the creative control that you will discover over your own life experience, we know that the greatest value of all will be the freedom that you will discover as you learn to apply the *Art of Allowing*.

Since the larger part of you already knows all of this, we see our work as reminding you of what, at some level, you already know. It is our expectation that as you read these words, if it is your desire you will be guided step-by-step to an Awakening—to a recognition of the *Total You*.

You Are Valuable to *All-That-Is*

It is our desire that you return to the understanding of the immense value that you are to *All-That-Is,* for you are truly on the Leading Edge of thought, adding unto the Universe with your every thought, word, and deed. You are not inferior Beings here trying to catch up, but instead, Leading-Edge creators with all of the resources of the Universe at your disposal.

We want you to know your value, for in the absence of that understanding, you do not attract the legacy that truly belongs to you. In your lack of self-appreciation, you deny yourself your natural inheritance of continuous joy. And while the Universe still benefits from everything that you experience, it is our desire that *you* begin to reap the fruits of your labor here and now, also.

It is our absolute knowing that you will find the keys that will lead you to the life experience that you intended even before you emerged into this body. We will assist you in fulfilling your life's purpose, and we know that this is important to you, for we hear you ask: *Why am I here? What can I do to make my life better? How do I know what is right?* And we are here to answer all of that in detail.

We are ready for your questions.

An Introduction to Being Well-Being

Jerry: What I would like, Abraham, is an introductory book, written especially for those people who want to have conscious control over their own life experiences. I would like for there to be enough information and guidance in this one book so that each reader could begin immediately using these ideas, and therefore immediately experience an increase in their state of happiness, or their state of Well-Being . . . understanding that they will probably want further clarification on some specific points later on.

Abraham: Everyone will begin from right where they are, and it is our expectation that those who are seeking will find the answers they are looking for here in this book. None of us can offer everything that we know, or want to convey, at any one point in time. And so, we will offer a clear basis of understanding the *Laws of the Universe* here, knowing that some will be interested in going beyond what is written, and some will not. Our work is continually evolving through the questions that are being asked as a result of the stimulation of what has been discussed before. There is no end to the evolution of that which we all are.

The *Universal Laws:* Defined

There are three *Eternal Universal Laws* that we want to assist you in understanding more clearly so that you may apply them intentionally, effectively, and satisfactorily through your physical expression of life. The *Law of Attraction* is the first of the *Laws* that we will offer, for if you do not understand, and are not able to effectively apply, the *Law of Attraction*, then the second *Law,* the *Science of Deliberate Creation*, and the third, the *Art of Allowing,* cannot be utilized. You must first understand and effectively utilize the first *Law* in order to understand and utilize the second. And you must be able to understand and utilize the second *Law* before you will be able to understand and utilize the third.

The first *Law,* the *Law of Attraction,* says: *That which is like unto itself, is drawn.* While this may seem like a rather simple statement, it defines the most powerful *Law* in the Universe—a *Law* that affects all things at all times. Nothing exists that is unaffected by this powerful *Law.*

The second *Law,* the *Science of Deliberate Creation,* says: *That which I give thought to and that which I believe or expect—is.* In short, you get what you are thinking about, whether you want it or not. A *deliberate* application of thought is really what the *Science of Deliberate Creation* is about, for if you do not understand these *Laws,* and deliberately apply them, then you may very well be creating by default.

The third *Law,* the *Art of Allowing,* says: *I am that which I am, and I am willing to allow all others to be that which they are.* When you are willing to allow others to be as they are, even in their not allowing of you, then you will be an *Allower,* but it is not likely that you will reach that point until you first come to understand *how* it is you get what you get.

Only when you understand that another cannot be a part of your experience unless you invite them in through your thoughts (or through your attention to them), and that circumstances cannot be a part of your experience unless you invite them to you through your thought (or through your observation of them), will you be the *Allower* that you wanted to be when you came forth into this expression of life.

An understanding of these three powerful *Universal Laws,* and a deliberate application of them, will lead you to the joyous freedom of being able to create your own life experience exactly as you want it to be. Once you understand that all people, circumstances, and events are invited into your experience by you, through your thought, you will begin to live your life as you intended when you made the decision to come forth into this physical body. And so, an understanding of the powerful *Law of Attraction,* coupled with an intention to *Deliberately Create* your own life experience, will ultimately lead you to the unparalleled freedom that can only come from a complete understanding and application of the *Art of Allowing.*

PART II

The *Law* of
Attraction

The Universal *Law of Attraction:* Defined

Jerry: Well, Abraham, I assume that the first subject that you will discuss with us in detail is the *Law of Attraction*. I know you've said that this is the most powerful *Law*.

Abraham: Not only is the *Law of Attraction* the most powerful *Law* in the Universe, but you must understand it before anything else that we offer will be of value. And you must understand it before anything you are living, or anything you observe anyone else living, will make any sense. Everything in your life and the lives of those around you is affected by the *Law of Attraction*. It is the basis of everything that you see manifesting. It is the basis of everything that comes into your experience. An awareness of the *Law of Attraction* and an understanding of how it works is essential to living life on purpose. In fact, it is essential to living the life of joy that you came forth to live.

The *Law of Attraction* says: *That which is like unto itself, is drawn.* When you say, "Birds of a feather flock together," you are actually talking about the *Law of Attraction*. You see it evidenced when you wake up feeling unhappy, and then throughout the day things get worse and worse, and at the end of the day you say, "I shouldn't have gotten out of bed." You see the *Law of Attraction* evidenced in your society when you see that the one who speaks most about illness has illness; when you see that the one who speaks most about prosperity has prosperity. The *Law of Attraction* is evident when you set your radio dial on 630AM and you *expect* to receive the broadcast from the transmitting tower of 630AM, because you understand that the radio signals between the transmitting tower and your receiver must *match.*

As you begin to understand—or better stated, as you begin to remember—this powerful *Law of Attraction,* the evidence of it that surrounds you will be easily apparent, for you will begin to recognize the exact correlation between what you have been thinking about and what is actually coming into your experience. Nothing merely shows up in your experience. *You attract it—all of it. No exceptions.*

Because the *Law of Attraction* is responding to the thoughts that you hold at all times, it is accurate to say that *you are creating your own reality.* Everything that you experience is attracted to you because the *Law of Attraction* is responding to the thoughts that you are offering. Whether you are remembering something from the past, observing something in your present, or imagining something about your future, the thought that you are focused upon in your powerful now has activated a vibration within you—and the *Law of Attraction* is responding to it now.

People often explain, in the midst of unwanted things occurring in their experience, that they are certain *they* did not create such a thing. "I wouldn't have done this unwanted thing to myself!" they explain. And while we know that you did not deliberately bring this unwanted thing into your experience, we must still explain that only *you* could have caused it, for no one else has the power to attract what comes to you but you. By focusing upon this unwanted thing, or the essence of it, you have created it by *default.* Because you did not understand the *Laws of the Universe,* or the rules of the game, so to speak, you have invited unwanted things into your experience through your attention to them.

*To better understand the <u>Law of Attraction</u>, see yourself as a mag-
net attracting unto you the essence of that which you are thinking and
feeling. And so, if you are feeling fat, you cannot attract thin. If you feel
poor, you cannot attract prosperity, and so on. It defies <u>Law.</u>*

Giving Thought to It Is Inviting It

*The more you come to understand the power of the <u>Law of Attraction</u>,
the more interest you will have in deliberately directing your thoughts—
for you get what you think about, whether you want it or not.*

*Without exception, that which you give thought to is that which you
begin to invite into your experience.* When you think a little thought
of something that you want, through the *Law of Attraction*, that
thought grows larger and larger, and more and more powerful.
When you think a thought of something you do not want, the *Law
of Attraction* draws unto it, and it grows larger and larger, also. And
so, the larger the thought grows, the more power it draws unto it,
and then the more certain you are to receive the experience.

When you see something you would like to experience and you
say, "Yes, I would like to have that," through your *attention* to it you
invite it into your experience. However, when you see something
that you do not want to experience and you shout, "No, no, I do
not want that!" through your *attention* to it you invite that into
your experience. In this attraction-based Universe, there is no such
thing as exclusion. Your attention to it includes it in your vibration,
and if you hold it in your attention or awareness long enough, the
Law of Attraction will bring it into your experience, for there is no
such thing as "No." To clarify, when you look at something and
shout, "No, I don't want to experience that; go away!" then what
you are actually doing is calling it into your experience, for there is
no such thing as "No" in an attraction-based Universe. Your attention to it says, "Yes, come to me, this thing I do *not* want!"

Fortunately, here in your physical time-space reality, things
do not manifest into your experience instantaneously. There is a
wonderful *buffer of time* between when you begin to think about
something and the time it manifests. That *buffer of time* gives you

the opportunity to redirect your attention more and more in the direction of the things that you actually do want to manifest in your experience. And long before it manifests (actually, when you first begin to give thought to it), you can tell by the way you *feel* whether it is something you want to manifest or not. If you continue to give your attention to it—whether it is something you want or something you do not want—it will come into your experience.

These *Laws,* even if you do not understand that they do, affect your experience even in your ignorance of them. And while you may not be aware of having heard of the *Law of Attraction*, its powerful effect is evident in every aspect of your life experience.

As you consider what you read here and begin to notice the correlation between what you are thinking and speaking and what you are getting, you will begin to understand the powerful *Law of Attraction*. And as you deliberately direct your thoughts and focus upon the things that you do want to draw into your experience, you will begin to receive the life experience that you desire on all subjects.

Your physical world is a vast and diverse place full of an amazing variety of events and circumstances, some of which you approve of (and would like to experience), and some of which you disapprove of (and would not like to experience). It was not your intention as you came forth into this physical experience to ask the world to change in order to accommodate your opinions of the way things should be, by eliminating all things that you do not approve of and adding to the things you *do* approve of.

You are here to create the world around you that you choose, while you allow the world—as others choose it to be—to exist, also. And while their choices in no way hinder your own choices, your attention to what they are choosing does affect your vibration, and therefore your own point of attraction.

My Thoughts Have Magnetic Power

The *Law of Attraction* and its magnetic power reaches out into the Universe and attracts other thoughts that are vibrationally like it . . . and brings that to you: Your attention to subjects, your activation of thoughts, and the *Law of Attraction's* response to those thoughts is responsible for every person, every event, and every circumstance that comes into your experience. All of these things are brought into your experience through a sort of powerful magnetic funnel as they are vibrational matches to your own thoughts.

You get the essence of what you are thinking about, whether it is something you want or something you do not want. That may be unsettling to you at first, but in time, it is our expectation that you will come to appreciate the fairness, the consistency, and the absoluteness of this powerful *Law of Attraction.* Once you understand this *Law* and begin to pay attention to what you are giving your attention to, you will regain control of your own life experience. And with that control you will again remember that there is nothing that you desire that you cannot *achieve,* and there is nothing that you do not want that you cannot release from your experience.

Understanding the *Law of Attraction* and recognizing the absolute correlation between what you have been thinking and feeling—and what is manifesting in your life experience—will cause you to be more aware of the stimulation of your own thoughts. You will begin to notice that your own thoughts may be stimulated from something you read or watch on television or hear or observe from someone else's experience. And once you see the effect that the *Law of Attraction* has upon these thoughts that begin small and grow larger and more powerful with your attention to them, you will feel a desire within you to begin to direct your thoughts to more of the things that you do want to experience. For whatever you are pondering, and no matter what the source of stimulation of that thought . . . as you ponder that thought, the *Law of Attraction* goes to work and begins to offer you other thoughts, conversations, and experiences that are of a similar nature.

Whether you are remembering the past, observing the present, or imagining the future, you are doing it right *now,* and whatever you are focusing upon is causing an activation of a vibration that the *Law of Attraction* is responding to. At first you may be privately pondering a particular subject, but if you think about it long enough, you will start to notice other people beginning to discuss it with you as the *Law of Attraction* finds others who are offering a similar vibration and brings them right to you. The longer you focus upon something, the more powerful it becomes; and the stronger that your *point of attraction* is to it, the more evidence of it appears in your life experience. *Whether you are focusing upon things you want or things you do not want, the evidence of your thoughts continually flows toward you.*

My *Inner Being* Communicates Through Emotion

You are much more than you see here in your physical body, for while you are, indeed, a wondrous *physical* creator, you exist, simultaneously, in another dimension. There is a part of you, a *Non-Physical* part of you—we call it your *Inner Being*—that exists right now while you are here in this physical body.

Your emotions are your physical indication of your relationship with your Inner Being. In other words, as you are focused upon a subject and have your specific perspective and opinion about it, your *Inner Being* is also focused upon it and has a perspective and opinion about it. The *emotions* that you feel are your indication of the match or mismatch of those opinions. For example, something may have happened and your current opinion of yourself is that you should have done better or that you are not smart, or that you are unworthy. Since the current opinion of your *Inner Being* is that you are doing fine, and that you are smart and eternally worthy, there is a definite mismatch in these opinions, and you would feel this mismatch in the form of *negative emotion.* On the other hand, when you feel proud of yourself or love yourself or someone else, your current opinion is a much closer match to what your *Inner Being* is feeling in the moment; and in that case, you would feel the *positive emotions* of pride, love, or appreciation.

Your *Inner Being,* or *Source Energy,* always offers a perspective that is to your greatest advantage, and when your perspective matches that, then positive attraction is occurring. In other words, the better you feel, the better your *point of attraction,* and the better things are turning out for you. The comparative vibrations of your perspective and that of your *Inner Being* are responsible for this magnificent *Guidance* that is always available to you.

Since the *Law of Attraction* is always responding to and acting on whatever vibration you are offering, it is extremely helpful to understand that your emotions are letting you know whether you are in the process of creating something you want or something you do not want.

Often, when our physical friends learn of the powerful *Law of Attraction* and begin to understand that they are attracting things to themselves by virtue of what they are thinking, they try to monitor each thought, often feeling guarded about their thoughts. But the monitoring of thoughts is a difficult thing because there are so many things that you might think about, and the *Law of Attraction* is continually bringing more.

Rather than trying to monitor your thoughts, we encourage you to simply pay attention to how you are feeling. For if you should choose a thought that is not in harmony with the way the broader, older, wiser, loving *Inner Being* part of you sees it, you will feel the discord, and then you can easily redirect your thought to something that feels better and which therefore serves you better.

You knew, when you made the decision to come forth into this physical body, that you would have access to this wonderful *Emotional Guidance System,* for you knew then that through your wonderful, ever-present emotions, you would be able to know if you were straying from your broader knowing or flowing with it.

When you are giving thought in a direction of something that you want, you will feel positive emotion. When you are giving thought in the direction of what you do not want, you will feel negative emotion. And so, simply by paying attention to the way you are feeling, you will know, at all times, the direction from which your powerful magnetic Being is attracting the subject of whatever you are giving thought to.

My Omnipresent *Emotional Guidance System*

Your wonderful *Emotional Guidance System* is a great advantage to you because the *Law of Attraction* is always working whether you know that it is or not. And so, whenever you are giving thought to something that you do *not* want, and you stay focused upon that thought, by *Law* you are attracting more and more and more and more, until eventually you will attract matching events or circumstances right into your experience.

However, if you are aware of your *Emotional Guidance System* and are sensitive to the way you feel, then you will notice, in the early, subtle stages, that you are focused upon something that you do *not* want, and you can easily change the thought to begin attracting something that you *do* want. If you are not sensitive to the way you are feeling, then you will not consciously notice that you are thinking in the direction of what you do not want, and you may very well attract something very large and powerful that you do not want that will be more difficult to deal with later.

When an idea occurs to you and you feel eagerness about it, that means that your *Inner Being* is a *vibrational match* to the idea, and your positive emotion is an indication that the vibration of your thought in this moment matches that of your *Inner Being*. That is, in fact, what *inspiration* is: You are, in the moment, a perfect vibrational match to the broader perspective of your *Inner Being*, and because of that alignment, you are now receiving clear communication, or *Guidance*, from your *Inner Being*.

What If I Want It to Happen More Quickly?

Because of the *Law of Attraction*, matching thoughts are drawn together, and as they do so, they become more powerful. And as they become more powerful—and therefore closer to manifestation—the emotion that you feel also becomes proportionately larger. When you are focused upon something that you desire, then through the *Law of Attraction*, more and more thoughts about what you desire will be drawn, and you will feel greater positive emotion. *You can speed the creation of something simply by giving it more attention—the Law of Attraction takes care of the rest and brings to you the essence of the subject of your thought.*

We would define the words *want* or *desire* as follows: *To focus attention, or give thought toward a subject, while at the same time experiencing positive emotion.* When you give your attention to a subject and you feel only positive emotion about it as you do so, it will come very quickly into your experience. Sometimes we hear our physical friends speaking the words *want* or *desire* while at the same time feeling *doubt* or *fear* that their desire cannot be achieved. From our point of view, it is not possible to purely desire something while feeling negative emotion.

Pure desire is always accompanied by positive emotion. Perhaps that is why people disagree with our use of the words *want* or *desire.* They often argue that "wanting" implies a sort of lack and contradicts its own meaning, and we agree. But the problem is not with the word or label itself, but instead, with the state of emotion expressed while using the word.

It is our desire to help you understand that you can get to wherever you want to be from wherever you are, no matter where you are or what your current state of Being. The most important thing to understand is that your mental state of Being, or your attitude, in the moment is the basis from which you will attract more. So, the powerful and consistent *Law of Attraction* is responding to everything in this vibrational Universe—bringing people with matching vibrations together, bringing situations with matching vibrations together, and bringing thoughts with matching vibrations together. Indeed, everything in your life, from the way thoughts roll across your mind, to the people you rendezvous with in traffic, is the way that it is, due to the *Law of Attraction.*

How Do I Want to See Myself?

For most of you, many things in your life are going well and you want a continuation of those things, but there are also things that you wish to be different. In order for things to change, you have to see them as you want them to be rather than continuing to observe them as they are. The majority of the thoughts that you probably think are about the things that you are observing, which means that *what-is* dominates your focus, attention, vibration, and therefore your *point of attraction*. That is further compounded as those around you also observe you.

And so, as a result of the overwhelming amount of attention that most of you give to your current situation *(what-is)*, change comes very slowly or not at all. A steady stream of different people flows into your life, but the essence or theme of those experiences does not change very much.

In order to effect true positive change in your experience, you must disregard how things are—as well as how others are seeing you—and give more of your attention to the way you prefer things to be. With practice, you will change your *point of attraction* and will experience a substantial change in your life experience. Sickness can become wellness, lack of abundance can become abundance, bad relationships can be replaced with good relationships, confusion can be replaced with clarity, and so on.

By deliberately directing your thoughts—rather than merely observing what is happening around you—you will begin to change the vibrational patterns to which the *Law of Attraction* is responding. And in time, with far less effort than you may currently believe, you will no longer—by responding to what others perceive you to be—be creating a future that is so similar to your past and present. Instead, you will be the powerful deliberate creator of your own experience.

You would not likely see a sculptor throwing his large wad of clay down onto his worktable exclaiming, "Oh, it didn't turn out right!" He knows that he must put his hands into his clay and work with it to mold it so that the vision in his mind matches the clay on his table. The variety of your life experience gives you the clay from which you will mold your life experience, and merely observing it as it is, without getting ahold of it and deliberately molding it to match your desires, is not satisfying—and is not what you had in mind when you made the decision to come into this time-space reality. We want you to understand that your "clay," no matter how it may look right now, is moldable. No exceptions.

Welcome, Little One, to Planet Earth

You may be feeling that it would be easier to be hearing these words if they had come to you on the first day of your experience upon this planet Earth. And if we were talking to you on your first day of physical life experience, this is what we would be saying:

Welcome, little one, to planet Earth. . . . There is nothing that you cannot be, do, or have. You are a magnificent creator, and you are here by virtue of your powerful and deliberate wanting to be here. You have specifically applied the wondrous <u>Science of Deliberate Creation</u>, and by your ability to do that, you are here.

Go forth, giving thought to what you want, attracting life experiences to help you decide what you want, and once you have decided, giving thought only unto that.

Most of your time will be spent collecting data—data that will help you decide what it is you want. . . . Your real work is to decide what you want and then focus upon it, for it is through focusing upon what you want that you will attract it. That is the process of creating: giving thought to what you want, so much thought, and such clear thought, that your <u>Inner Being</u> offers forth emotion. And as you are giving thought, with emotion, you become the most powerful of all magnets. That is the process by which you will attract what you want into your experience.

Many of the thoughts that you will be thinking will not be powerful in their attracting, not in the beginning—not unless you stay focused upon them long enough that they become more. For as they become more in quantity, they become more in power. And as they are becoming more in quantity and more in power, the emotion that you will be feeling from your <u>Inner Being</u> will be greater.

When you think thoughts that bring forth emotion, you are accessing the power of the Universe. Go forth (we would say) *on this first day of life experience, knowing that your work is to decide what you want—and then to focus upon that.*

But we are not talking to you on the first day of your life experience. You have been here for a while. Most of you have been seeing yourself, not only through your own eyes (in fact, not even primarily through your own eyes), but through the eyes of others; therefore, *many of you are not now currently in the state of Being that you want to be.*

Is My "Reality" Really All That Real?

We intend to offer you a process whereby you can achieve the state of Being that is of your choosing so that you can access the power of the Universe and begin attracting the subject of your *wanting,* rather than the subject of what you feel is your actual state of Being. For, from our perspective, *there is a very great difference between that which now exists—which you call your "reality"—and that which your reality really is.*

Even if you sit in a body that is not healthy or in one that is not of the size, shape, or vitality that you choose; in a lifestyle that does not please you; driving an automobile that embarrasses you; interacting with others who do not bring you pleasure . . . we want to assist you in understanding that while that may seem to be your state of Being, it need not be. *Your state of Being is the way you feel about yourself at any point in time.*

How Can I Increase My Magnetic Power?

The thoughts that you think without bringing forth the feeling of strong emotion are not of great magnetic power. In other words, while every thought that you think has creative potential, or magnetic attracting potential, the thoughts that are thought in combination with the feeling of strong emotion are the most powerful. Certainly, the majority of your thoughts, then, have no great attracting power. They are more or less maintaining what you have already attracted.

And so, can you not see the value of spending 10 or 15 minutes every day deliberately setting forth powerful thoughts that evoke great, powerful, passionate, positive emotion in order to attract circumstances and events into your life experience that are to your wanting? (We see great value in that.)

Here we will offer a process by which you may spend a little bit of time every day intentionally attracting into your experience the health, vitality, prosperity, positive interaction with others . . . all the things that make up your vision of what the perfect life experience would be for you. And that will be a changing thing, friends. For as you intend and receive, you will not only receive the benefit of that which you have created, but you will also receive a new perspective from which your intentions will be different. That is what evolution and growth are about.

Abraham's *Creative Workshop Process*

Here is the process: You are going to go to a kind of *Creative Workshop* every day—not for a long period of time—15 minutes is a good amount of time; 20 minutes at most. This *Workshop* need not occur in the same place in every day, but it is good if it is a place where you will not be distracted or interrupted. This is not a place where you will enter an altered state of consciousness; it is not a meditative state. It is a state of giving thought to what you want with such clarity that your *Inner Being* responds by offering confirming emotion.

Before you begin this process, it is important that you be happy, for if you go there unhappy or feeling no emotion, then your work will not be of great value, for your attracting power will not be there. When we say "happy," we are not speaking of that jumping-up-and-down sort of excitement. We mean an uplifted, lighthearted feeling, that sort of sensation where all is well. And so, we recommend that you do whatever it takes to get happy. For each of you it is a different process. . . . For Esther, hearing music is a very fast way to get that uplifted, joyous feeling—but not all music accomplishes this, and not even the same music every time. For some of you it is interacting with animals or being near moving water, but once you bring yourself to that good feeling, then sit—and now your *Workshop* has begun.

Your job here in this *Workshop* is to assimilate data that you have been collecting from your real-life experiences (as you have been interacting with others and moving in and out of your physical environment). Your work here is to bring the data together in a sort of picture of yourself, one that satisfies and pleases you.

Your life experience outside of your *Workshop* will be of great value, for as you are moving around through your day, no matter what you are doing—going to work; working around your home; interacting with your mate or your friends or your children or your parents—*if you will use your time, with one of your intentions being to collect data and look for things that you like that you may bring into your* <u>Workshop</u>—*then you will find that every day is one of fun.*

Have you ever gone on a shopping spree where you had some money in your pocket and your intent was to find something to buy? And as you were looking around, although there were many things that you did not want, your intent was to find something that you *did* want to exchange for the money. Well, that is the way we would like you to look at every day of your life experience . . . as if you have a pocketful of something that you are exchanging for this data that you are collecting.

For example, you may see someone who has a joyful personality. Collect that data, intending to bring it into your *Workshop* later. You may see someone driving a vehicle that you would like; collect that data. You may see an occupation that pleases you. . . . Whatever it is that you are seeing that pleases you, remember it. (You could even write it down.) As you see anything that you think you would like to be in your life experience, see yourself collecting that data in a sort of mental bank. And then when you go into your *Workshop,* you can begin assimilating the data, and as you do so, *you will prepare a picture of yourself from which you will begin attracting into your experience the essence of that which has been pleasing you.*

If you are able to grasp the knowledge that your *real* work—no matter what other activities you are performing—is to look around for things that you want with the intent of bringing them into your *Workshop* in order to create your vision of yourself from which you will attract—then you will come to know that there is nothing that you cannot be, do, or have.

I Am Now in My *Creative Workshop*

And so now you are feeling happy, and you are sitting someplace in your *Workshop*. Here is an example of the work you may do in your *Creative Workshop:*

I like being here; I recognize the value and power of this time. I feel very good to be here.

I see myself in a sort of total package, one that I know is of my own creating, and certainly a package of my choosing. I am full of energy in this picture of myself—tireless, and really moving through life experience without resistance. As I see myself gliding about, moving in and out of my car, in and out of buildings, in and out of rooms, in and out of conversations, and in and out of life experiences, I see myself flowing effortlessly, comfortably, and happily.

I see myself attracting only those who are in harmony with my current intent. And I am clearer and clearer in every moment about what it is I want. When I get into my automobile and I am moving to a place, I see myself arriving healthy and refreshed and on time, and prepared for whatever it is that I am about to do there. I see myself dressed to perfection in just the manner that I choose for myself. And it is nice to know that it matters not what others are choosing, or what others are even <u>thinking</u> about what I am choosing.

What is important is that I am pleased with me, and as I see myself, I certainly am.

I recognize that I am unlimited in all facets of my life. . . . I have a bank account balance that is unlimited, and as I see myself moving through life experiences, it is exhilarating to know that there is nothing that I am choosing that is limited by money. I am making all of my decisions based upon whether I want the experience or not—not based upon whether or not I can <u>afford</u> the experience. For I know I am a magnet who attracts, at any point, whatever prosperity, health, and relationships I choose.

I choose absolute and continuing abundance, for I understand that there is no limit to the abundance in the Universe, and that by my attracting abundance to myself I am not limiting another. . . . There is enough for everyone. The key is for each of us to see it and want it—and then we will each attract it. And so, I have chosen "unlimited," not necessarily putting a big stash away—for I understand that I have the power to attract it as I want it for whatever I want it for. And as I think of something else that I want, the money flows to me easily, so I have an unlimited supply of abundance and prosperity.

There are abundant aspects in every area of my life. . . . I see myself surrounded by others who, like me, want growth; and who are drawn to me by my willingness to allow them to be, do, or have whatever they want while I do not need to draw into my experience those things that they may be choosing that I do not like. I see myself interacting with others; and talking, laughing, and enjoying that which is perfect in them while they enjoy that which is perfect in me. All of us are appreciating one another, and none of us is criticizing or noticing those things that we do not like.

I see myself in perfect health. I see myself in absolute prosperity. I see myself invigorated with life, again appreciating this physical life experience that I wanted so very much as I decided to be a physical Being. It is glorious to be here as a physical Being, making decisions with my physical brain but accessing the power of the Universe through the power of the <u>Law of Attraction</u>. And it is from this marvelous state of Being that I now attract more of the same. It is good. It is fun. I like it very much.

I will leave this <u>Workshop</u>, and I will set out—during the remainder of this day—to look for more things that I like. It is nice to know that if I see one who is prosperous, but sick, I do not need to bring the whole package into my <u>Workshop</u>, just the part that I like. So I will bring the example of prosperity, and I will leave out the example of sickness. My work, for now, is done.

Are Not All *Laws* Universal *Laws?*

Jerry: Abraham, you spoke to us of three major *Universal Laws.* Are there some *Laws* that are not *Universal?*

Abraham: There are many that you may call *Laws.* We reserve our definition of *Law* for those things that are *Universal.* In other words, as you enter into this physical dimension, you have the agreement of time, the agreement of gravity, and the agreement of this perception of space; but those agreements are not *Universal,* for there are other dimensions that do not share those experiences. In many cases, where you may use the word *Law,* we would use the word *agreement,* instead. There are no other *Universal Laws* that we are waiting to divulge to you later.

How Do I Best Utilize the *Law of Attraction?*

Jerry: Are there many different ways that we can consciously or deliberately use this *Law of Attraction?*

Abraham: We will begin by saying that you are *always* utilizing it, whether you know that you are or not. You cannot stop using it, for it is inherent in everything that you do. But we appreciate your question, for you want to understand how to *deliberately* use it for the achievement of that which you *intentionally* desire.

Being aware that the *Law of Attraction* exists is the most important part of utilizing it deliberately. Since the *Law of Attraction* is always responding to your thoughts, a deliberate focusing of your thought is important.

Choose subjects that are of interest to you, and think about them in a way that benefits you. In other words, look for the *positive aspects* of the subjects that are important to you. As you choose a thought, the *Law of Attraction* will act upon it, attracting more thoughts like it, thus making that thought more powerful.

By staying focused on a subject of your choosing, your point of attraction *on that topic will become much more powerful than if your mind moves from subject to subject. There is tremendous power in focusing.*

As you make deliberate choices about the thoughts you think, the things you do, and even the people you spend time with, you will feel the benefit of the *Law of Attraction.* When you spend time with others who appreciate you, it stimulates your own thoughts of appreciation. When you spend time with those who see your flaws, then their perception of your flaws often becomes your *point of attraction.*

As you come to realize that whatever you are giving your attention to is getting larger (because the *Law of Attraction* says that it must), you may become more particular about those things that you give your initial attention to. It is much easier to change the direction of your thoughts in the early stages of the thought before the thought has gathered much momentum. But it is possible to change the direction of your thought at any time.

Can I Instantly Reverse My Creative Momentum?

Jerry: Let's say there are those who already have something going on, from their previous thoughts, and now they decide they want to suddenly change the direction of their creation. Isn't there a momentum factor? Don't they have to first slow down what's already in the process of being created? Or can they instantly create in a different direction?

Abraham: There is a momentum factor caused by the *Law of Attraction*. The *Law of Attraction* says: *That which is like unto itself, is drawn.* So whatever thought you have activated by your attention to it is getting bigger. But we want you to realize that the gathering of momentum is a gradual thing. And so, rather than trying to turn that thought around, consider focusing upon another thought.

Let us say you have been thinking about something that you do not want, and you have been doing that for a while, so you have a rather strong negative momentum going. It would not be possible for you to suddenly begin thinking the opposite thought. In fact, from where you are standing, you would not even have access to those kinds of thoughts—*but you could choose a thought that feels slightly better than the thoughts you have been thinking, and then another, and then another, until gradually you could change the direction of your thoughts.*

Another effective process for changing the direction of your thought is to change the subject altogether, deliberately looking for the positive aspect of something. If you are able to do that, and if you are willing to try to stay focused upon that better-feeling thought for a while, then, since the *Law of Attraction* is now responding to that thought, the balance of your thoughts is now improved. Now when you go back to revisit your previous negative thought, since you are now in a different mode of vibration, that thought will be slightly affected by your vibrational improvement. Little by little you will improve the vibrational content of the subject that you choose to think about, and as that happens, everything in your life begins to shift in a more positive direction.

How Can a Person Overcome Disappointment?

Jerry: For the individual who is trying to make a severe switch in the positive direction of their prosperity, or of their health, if they already had a momentum factor going the other way, how much faith or belief would it require for them to overcome their disappointment and say, "Well, I know this is going to work out for me," even though it hasn't worked yet?

Abraham: You see, from your point of disappointment, you are attracting more to be disappointed about. . . . An understanding of the process of creation is really the best way. That is the value of the *Creative Workshop,* of getting happy, and then going to a place where you *see* it as you are wanting it to be; seeing it until you are believing it so clearly that it is already bringing forth emotion—and from *that* state of Being, you will attract it as you want it to be.

Disappointment *is communication from your <u>Inner Being</u> letting you know that that which you are focused upon is not what you want. If you are sensitive to the way that you are feeling, then the disappointment itself will let you know that what you are thinking about is not what you want to experience.*

What Causes Worldwide Waves of Unwanted Events?

Jerry: Over the years, I've seen TV newscasts, or whatever, that report the hijacking of an airplane or a terrorist act or a severe case of child abuse or a mass murder or something negative like that—and then I'll see an almost worldwide wave of those events beginning to occur. Is that brought on by the same process?

Abraham: Attention to any subject amplifies it because attention to the subject activates the vibration of it and the *Law of Attraction* responds to the activated vibration.

Those who may be planning the hijacking of an airplane are adding power to that thought, but those who are *frightened* by the prospect of a hijacking are also adding power to the thought—for you add power to those things you do not want through your attention to them. Those who have a clear intent to not draw any sort of negative information into their experience are probably not watching the broadcast to begin with, you see.

There are so many different intentions and combinations of intentions that it is very difficult for us to point out, in general, how one would bring it about. . . . Certainly, these newscasts add to these situations. For as more and more people are focused upon what they are not wanting, they are adding to the creation of what they do not want. Their emotional power is adding great influence to the overall events of your world. That is what mass consciousness is about.

Can Attention to Medical Procedures Attract More?

Jerry: Currently, there's a wide range of televised surgery going on. Do you see that sort of thing as increasing the amount of surgery that will actually occur per capita? In other words, when individuals observe televised medical procedures, can they automatically become more of a vibrational match to the essence of medical procedures?

Abraham: When you give your attention to something, your potential for attracting it is increased. The more vivid the details, the more attention you will give it, and the more likely you are to attract it into your experience. And any negative emotion that you feel as you watch such a thing is your indication that you are negatively attracting.

Of course, the illness does not come upon you immediately, so you often do not make the correlation between your thoughts, your subsequent negative emotion, and the resulting illness, but they are absolutely linked together. *Your attention to anything is drawing it closer to you.*

Fortunately, because of the *buffer of time,* your thoughts do not become reality instantaneously, so you have ample opportunity to evaluate the direction of your thought (by the way you are feeling) and to change the direction of your thought whenever you find yourself feeling negative emotion.

The steady offering of details of illness is very influential in the increasing of sickness in your society. If you allow yourself to focus upon the constant barrage of unpleasant statistics regarding the never-ending stream of possible physical maladies, it cannot help but affect your personal *point of attraction.*

You might, instead, find a way of focusing your attention on those things that you *do* want to draw into your experience, for whatever you are consistently looking at, you are attracting. . . . *The more you think about illness and worry about illness—the more you attract illness.*

Should I Seek the Cause of My Negative Emotions?

Jerry: Suppose you are using the *Creative Workshop Process* of focusing on the things that you want, but then later, if you are out of the *Workshop* and you feel a negative emotion, would you suggest trying to find out what thought caused the negative emotion? Or would you suggest just thinking of one of the things that you'd been thinking about in the *Workshop* that you want?

Abraham: The power of the *Creative Workshop Process* is that the more attention you give to a subject, the more powerful it becomes, the easier it is to think about it, and the more of it begins to appear in your experience. Whenever you are aware that you are feeling negative emotion, it is important to understand that while you may not be aware of it, you have been conducting a negative *Workshop.*

Whenever you catch yourself feeling negative emotion, we would suggest that you try to gently pull your thoughts around to something that you *do* want to experience, and little by little you will change your habit of thought regarding those things. Whenever you are able to identify something that you do *not* want, you can always then identify what is it that you *do* want. And as you do that again and again, your pattern of thought—on every subject that is important to you—will shift more in the direction of what you do want. In other words, you will gradually build bridges from any current beliefs that are about things you do *not* want over to beliefs about things you *do* want.

An Example of Bridging an Unwanted Belief

Jerry: Can you provide an example of what you mean by "bridging a belief"?

Abraham: Your *Emotional Guidance System* works best when you are setting forth continual, deliberate intentions of what you desire. So let us say that you have intended, in your *Workshop,* perfect health; you've visualized yourself as a healthy, vital Being. And now you are moving through your day, and while having lunch you are sitting with a friend who is discussing her own illness. As she speaks about her illness, you find yourself feeling very uncomfortable and uneasy in the conversation. . . . Now, what is happening is, your *Guidance System* is indicating to you that *that which you are hearing and that which you are thinking—that which your friend is speaking—is not in harmony with your intent.* And then you make a very clear decision to stop this conversation from going any further in the direction of illness. And so you attempt to change the subject, but your friend is very excited and emotionally drawn to this topic, and she brings the conversation back to her illness. Again, your *Guidance System's* warning bells begin to ring.

The reason why you are feeling negative emotion is not only because your friend is talking about something that you do not want. *Your negative emotion is your indication that you hold beliefs that are contrary to your own desire.* Your friend's conversation merely activated beliefs within you that challenge your desire for wellness. So walking away from your friend and from this conversation will not change those beliefs. It is necessary that you start, right where you are, in the midst of that belief, and move it gradually, building a bridge, so to speak, to a belief that is more in harmony with your desire for wellness.

It is helpful, whenever you feel negative emotion, to stop and acknowledge what you were thinking about when the negative emotion surfaced. Whenever you feel negative emotion, it is always telling you that whatever you are thinking about is important, and that you are thinking about the opposite of what you really desire. So questions such as "What was I thinking about when this negative emotion surfaced?" and "What is it that I do want regarding this?" will help you realize that you are, in this moment, focused in direct opposition to what you really do want to attract into your experience.

For example: "What was I thinking about when this negative emotion surfaced? I was thinking about this being the flu season, and I was remembering how very sick I have been in the past with the flu. Not only did I miss work, and many other things that I wanted to do, but I felt miserable for so many days. What is it that I *do* want? I want to remain healthy this year."

But merely saying "I want to remain healthy" is usually not sufficient under these conditions because your memory of having the flu and therefore your belief about the probability of getting the flu are much stronger than your desire to remain well.

We would attempt to bridge our belief in this way:

This is usually the time of year that I get the flu.
I don't want to get the flu this year.
I hope I don't get the flu this year.
It seems like everyone gets it.
That may be an exaggeration. Everyone doesn't get the flu.
In fact, there have been many flu seasons when I didn't get the flu.
I don't always get the flu.

It's possible that this flu season could come and go without touching me at all.

I like the idea of being healthy.

Those past flu experiences came before I realized that I can control my experience.

Now that I understand the power of my own thoughts, things have changed.

Now that I understand the power of the Law of Attraction, things have changed.

It isn't necessary for me to experience the flu this year.

It isn't necessary for me to experience anything that I don't want.

It's possible for me to direct my thoughts toward things I do want to experience.

I like the idea of guiding my life to things that I do want to experience.

Now you have bridged the belief. If the negative thought returns—and it may continue to do so for a while—just guide your thoughts more deliberately, and eventually it will not come up again.

Are My Thoughts in My Dreams, Creating?

Jerry: I would like to understand the dream world. Are we creating in our dreams? Are we attracting anything through the thoughts that we're having or experiencing in our dreams?

Abraham: You are not. While you sleep, you have withdrawn your consciousness from your physical time-space reality, and you are temporarily not attracting while you are sleeping.

Whatever you are thinking (and therefore feeling) and that which you are attracting is always a match. Also, what you are thinking and feeling in the dream state and what is manifesting in your life experience is always a match. *Your dreams give you a glimpse into what you have created or what you are in the process of creating—but you are not in the process of creating while you are dreaming.*

Often you are unaware of the pattern of your thoughts until they actually manifest in your experience because you have developed your habit of thought gradually over a long period of time. And while it is possible, even after something unwanted has manifested, to focus and change it to something you do want, it is more difficult to do that after it has manifested. An understanding of what your dream state really is can help you recognize the direction of your thoughts before they actually materialize in your experience. *It is much easier to correct the direction of your thoughts when your dream is your indication than it is when a real-life manifestation is your indication.*

Must I Take Their Good and Their Bad?

Jerry: To what degree are we a part of what someone whom we're associated with has attracted (wanted or unwanted)? In other words, how much does another person whom we're associated with bring into our life what they've attracted—the things that we want or the things that we don't want?

Abraham: Nothing can come into your life without your attention to it. Most people, however, are not very selective about the aspects of others to which they give their attention. In other words, if you notice *everything* about someone else, then you are inviting *all* of those aspects into your experience. If you give your attention only to the things you like most about them, you will invite into your experience only those things.

If someone is in your life, you have attracted them. And while it is sometimes difficult to believe, you also attract everything about your experience with them—for nothing can come into your experience without your personal attraction of it.

Should I "Resist Not, Evil"?

Jerry: So we don't really need to repel any negatives? We only have to attract what we want?

Abraham: It is not possible to push things that you do not want away from you, because in your pushing against them you are actually activating the vibration of them and therefore attracting them. Everything in this Universe is attraction based. In other words, there is no such thing as exclusion. When you shout "No!" at those things you do not want, you are actually inviting those unwanted things into your experience. When you shout "Yes!" at those things you do want, you are actually inviting those wanted things into your experience.

Jerry: That's where that saying "Resist ye not evil" probably came from.

Abraham: *If you are resisting anything, you are focused upon it, pushing against it, and activating the vibration of it—and therefore attracting it.* And so, it would not be a good idea to do that with anything that you do not want. "Resist ye not evil" would also be spoken by someone wise enough to understand that what humans call "evil" does not exist.

Jerry: Abraham, what would be your definition of the word *evil?*

Abraham: There would be no reason for the word *evil* to be in our vocabulary because there is nothing that we are aware of that we would label with the word. When humans use the word, they usually mean "that which opposes good." We have noticed that when humans use the word *evil,* they mean something that opposes *their* idea of what is good, or what is God. *Evil* is that which one believes is not in harmony with what they want.

Jerry: And *good?*

Abraham: *Good* is that which one believes they do want. You see, good and evil are only ways of defining *wanted* and *unwanted*. And *wanted* and *unwanted* only apply to the individual doing the wanting. It gets tricky when humans get involved in the wanting of others, and even trickier when they attempt to *control* the desires of others.

How Do I Find Out What I Really Want?

Jerry: One of the most common concerns I've heard over the years is people saying, "Well, I just don't know what I want." How *do* we know what we want?

Abraham: You have come forth into this physical life experience with the intention of experiencing the variety and contrast for the very purpose of determining your own personal preferences and desires.

Jerry: Could you give us an idea of a process we could use to find out what we want?

Abraham: Your life experience is continually helping you identify what you want. Even as you are keenly aware of something that you *do not* want, in that moment you are becoming more clear about that which you *do* want. And it is helpful to make the statement "I want to know what I want," because in your conscious awareness of that intention, the attraction process is intensified.

Jerry: So the person who's telling me "I want to know what I want," is, at that moment, beginning to find out what they want?

Abraham: Through the experience of life, you cannot help but identify, from your perspective, your personal opinions and preferences: "I prefer that to this, I like that more than this, I want to experience this, I don't want to experience that." You cannot help but come to your own conclusions as you sift through the details of your own life experience.

We do not believe that people are having such a difficult time deciding what they want as much as they do not believe that they can receive what they want. . . . Because they have not understood the powerful *Law of Attraction,* and because they have not been consciously aware of their own vibrational offering, they have not experienced any conscious control over the things that have come into their own experience. Many have experienced the discomfort of really wanting something and working very hard to try to achieve it, only to continue to hold it away because they were offering thoughts of the lack of it more predominantly than thoughts of the receiving of it. So, over time, they begin to associate the receiving of wanted things with hard work, struggle, and disappointment.

So when they say, "I don't know what I want," what they really mean is, "I don't know how to get what I want," or "I'm not willing to do what I think I need to do to try to get what I want," and "I really don't want to work so hard again only to have the discomfort of still not getting what I want!"

To make the statement "I want to know what I want!" is a first and powerful step in *Deliberate Creation.* But then, a deliberate directing of your attention to the things you want to attract into your experience must come next.

Most people have not been deliberately directing their thoughts toward the things that they really want, but instead, are simply observing whatever is going on around them. So when they see something that pleases them, they feel positive emotion, but when they see something that displeases them, they feel negative emotion. *Few realize that they can control the way they feel and positively affect the things that come into their life experience by deliberately directing their thoughts. But because they are not accustomed to doing that, it takes practice.* That is the reason why we encourage the *Creative Workshop Process.* By deliberately directing your thoughts and by creating pleasing mental scenarios in your own mind that induce good-feeling emotions within you, you begin to change your own *point of attraction.*

The Universe, which is responding to the thoughts that you are thinking, does not distinguish between a thought brought about by your observation of some reality you have witnessed and a thought brought about by your imagination. In either case, the thought equals your <u>point of attraction</u>—and if you focus upon it long enough, it will become your reality.

I Wanted Blue and Yellow but Got Green

When you are clear about *everything* that you want, you will get *all* of the results that you want. But often you are not completely clear. You say, for example, "I want the color yellow, and I want the color blue." But what you end up with is green. And then you say, "How did I get green? I did not intend that at all." But, it came forth as a blending of other intentions, you see. (Of course, blending the color yellow with the color blue creates the color green.)

And so, in a similar manner (at an unconscious level), there is a blending of intentions that is continually occurring within you, but it is so complex that your conscious thinking mechanism cannot sort it all out. But your *Inner Being can* sort it out—and can offer you guiding emotions. All that is required is that you pay attention to the way you feel, and that you let yourself be drawn to those things that feel good or right to you while you let yourself be moved away from those things that do not.

When you have practiced clarifying your intentions a bit, you will find yourself, in the very early stages of interacting with others, knowing whether what they are offering is of value or not. You will know whether you want to invite them into your experience or not.

How Does the Victim Attract the Robber?

Jerry: I can understand robbers being attracted to those they're robbing, but it's difficult to see innocent victims (as they're called) *attracting* the robbery, or the person being discriminated against *attracting* the prejudice.

Abraham: But they are, just the same. The assaulted and the assaulter are co-creators of the event.

Jerry: So, one of them is thinking about what they *don't* want and getting *it*, and the other is thinking about what they *do* want and getting (the vibrational essence of) that. In other words, they are, what you call, a vibrational match?

Abraham: It makes no difference whether you want the specifics of it or not; it is the vibrational essence of the subject of your attention that is attracted. *That which you really, really want, you get—and that which you really, really do not want, you get.*

The only way to avoid developing a powerful emotional thought about something is by not thinking the first not-so-powerful thought that is then added to by the *Law of Attraction.*

Let us say you read in the paper that someone has been robbed. Unless you read a detailed account that brings forth great emotion within you, reading the account or hearing about it will not necessarily put you in the attracting mode. But if you read about it or see it on television or discuss it with another until you begin to feel an emotional response about it, then you begin to draw a similar experience closer to you.

As you hear the statistics of what percentage of your population will be robbed this year, you must understand that the numbers are so high and getting higher because so many people are being stimulated by the thought. Those *warnings* do not protect you from robberies, but instead make them more likely. They do such a good job of making you aware of the prevalence of robberies, bringing that awareness to your attention again and again, that you not only think of it with emotion—but you expect it. *It is no wonder that you get so many of the things you do not want—you give so much of your attention to the things you do not want. . . .*

We would recommend that if you hear of an assault, you say, "That is their experience. I do not choose that." And then release the thought of what you *do not* want, and think of what you *do* want, because *you get what you think about, whether you want it or not.*

You came into this environment with so many others because you wanted the wonderful experience of co-creating. You can attract from your population those people with whom you would like to positively create, and you can attract from the people in your life the experiences you would like to create. *It is not necessary, or possible, to hide from or avoid unwanted people or experiences—but it is possible to attract only the people and experiences that please you.*

I Decided to Improve My Life

Jerry: I recall that, as a kid, I had extremely poor health and my body was very weak; and then as a teenager, I decided to, and did, build up my body strength, and I learned how to defend myself. I practiced martial arts and got very good at self-defense.

From the time I was a teenager until I was 33 years old, there was seldom a week that went by that I didn't have what we used to call a "fistfight," that I didn't hit somebody in the head. Then, in my 33rd year, after reading (in *The Talmudic Anthology*) about the counterproductivity of taking revenge, I made some major decisions, and one of them was that I was going to stop taking revenge—and since then I have not had to hit one person. In other words, all those people that I believed were picking on others and starting fights with me—from the day that I stopped practicing fighting (physically and mentally), those fight-provoking people stopped coming into my experience.

Abraham: So in your 33rd year you changed the direction of your attraction. You see, through the process of living your life and having those fights, week in and week out, you were coming to many conclusions about what you wanted and what you did not want. And while you may not have been consciously aware, with every fight you experienced you were getting clearer about not wanting that experience.

You did not like being hurt; you did not like hurting others; and even though you always felt completely justified in your reason for fighting, clear preferences were being born within you. The attraction of the book you mentioned came about because of those intentions. And as you read the book, it answered the questions that had been formulating within you at many levels of your Being. And as those answers came, a new intention was clarified, and a new *point of attraction* was born within you.

What's Behind Our Religious and Racial Prejudices?

Jerry: Why is there prejudice?

Abraham: It is often felt that there are those who do not like certain characteristics about other Beings, so in their dislike of those characteristics, they are responsible for the prejudice. We want to point out that it is not only the doing of the one who is accused of being prejudiced. More often, the one who *feels* discriminated against is the most powerful creator in that experience.

The Being who feels that others do not like him—for whatever reason—whether it is religion, race, gender, or social status . . . no matter what the reason is that he feels that he is being discriminated against—it is his attention to the subject of the prejudice that attracts his trouble.

Do "Likes Attract," or Do "Opposites Attract"?

Jerry: Abraham, there's a statement that doesn't seem to blend with what we've heard from you. And that statement is "Opposites attract." That seems different from what you teach, as far as "like attracting like." For instance, opposites do seem to attract, like an outgoing man will marry a shy woman, or an outgoing woman will be attracted to a shy man.

Abraham: Everything you see and everyone you know is offering vibrational signals, and those signals must match before attraction can take place. So even in a situation where people seem to be different, there must be a dominant basis of vibrational similarity for them to be together. It is *Law.* Within all people there are vibra-tions of that which is wanted and vibrations of the lack of what is wanted, and everything that comes into their experience always matches the vibrations that are dominant. No exceptions.

Let us introduce the word *harmony.* When two are exactly the same, then their intentions cannot be fulfilled. In other words, one who wants to sell does not do well to attract another seller. But the attracting of a buyer brings forth the *harmony.*

The shy man attracts an outgoing woman because his *intention* is to be more outgoing, so he is actually attracting the *subject* of his intention.

The magnetized skillet, whose essence is of iron, will attract to itself another object whose essence is of iron (that is, a bolt or a nail or another iron skillet) but it will not attract a skillet that is made of copper or aluminum.

When you set your radio receiver to the frequency of 98.7FM, you cannot pick up the signal of 630AM being broadcast from a radio tower. Those frequencies must match.

There is no vibrational evidence, anywhere in the Universe, that supports the idea that opposites attract. They do not.

Oposites do not attract

What about When What Felt Good Now Feels Bad?

Jerry: How is it that some people seem to eventually attract something they've really, really wanted, but then when it comes, they find that it turns out to be a very negative situation? It brings them pain.

Abraham: Often, from a place that is very far from what is wanted, people will decide what they do want. But instead of focus-ing upon that desire, and practicing the vibration of it until they have achieved vibrational alignment with their true desire—and allowing the *Law of Attraction* to then reach out into the Universe and bring them perfect matching results—they become impatient and try to *make* it happen by jumping into action. But when they take action before they have improved the content of their vibration,

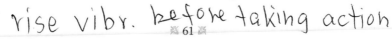
rise vibr. before taking action

what they get is something that matches their current vibration instead of something that matches their desire.

Until you practice your vibration, there is often a big gap between the vibration of what you actually want and the vibration that you are offering. However, without exception, what comes to you matches the vibration that you are offering.

For example, let us say that a woman has recently come from a bad relationship where her partner has verbally and physically abused her. She did not want that or like that. In fact she hated the life that she lived with that person. So, from her place of really knowing what she does *not* want, she makes a clear statement of what she *does* want. She wants a partner who loves her and treats her with kindness and respect. But she feels very insecure without a partner, and she wants a new partner immediately. And so, she goes someplace where she is accustomed to going and meets a new person who seems nice enough. But what she may not realize is that the *Law of Attraction* is still matching her up with whatever is dominant within her. And right now, what is still dominant within her is the vibration of what she does not want because the unwanted parts of her last relationship are much more active within her thoughts than the new intentions that have been established. In her eagerness to soothe her feelings of insecurity, she takes action and jumps into this new relationship—and gets *more* of what is dominant within her vibration.

It would be our encouragement that she take things more slowly and spend more time thinking about what she wants until those thoughts are the basis for the dominant vibration within her. And then, let the *Law of Attraction* bring her wonderful new partner to her.

Jerry: Okay, that makes sense. It's sort of like we used to say: "They got some things they hadn't bargained for."

Abraham: That is the value of the *Creative Workshop Process.* When you get into your *Workshop,* visualizing *all* of the wonderful possibilities, letting your emotion come forth when you are touching upon that which you are really wanting, and then working upon staying focused where it feels good, then you will not have so much of that. You will discover how to make what you *do* want your most dominant vibration, and then when the *Law of Attraction* matches those thoughts that you have been practicing, you will not be surprised. In fact, you will begin to recognize (the manifestation of) the wonderful things that you have been practicing in your mind.

Is Everything Composed of Thought?

Jerry: Is everything and everyone composed *of* thought or *by* thought? Or neither?

Abraham: Both. Thought can be attracted by other thoughts through the power of the *Law of Attraction*. Thought is the vibration that the *Law of Attraction* is acting upon. Thought is the stuff, or the manifestation, and it is also the vehicle through which all things are attracted or created.

See your world as a sort of well-stocked kitchen where every possible ingredient that has ever been pondered, considered, thought of, or wanted exists in an abundant, never-ending quantity; and see yourself as the chef, soliciting forth from the shelves of your kitchen whatever ingredients, in whatever quantity, you desire, and you are mixing it all together for the creation of your cake, which currently pleases you.

I Want More Joy, Happiness, and Harmony

Jerry: What if someone would say to you, "Abraham, I want to be more joyful. How can I use what you're teaching to attract more joy, happiness, and harmony into my life?"

Abraham: First, we would compliment the person on discovering the most important desire of all: *the seeking of joy.* For in seeking and finding joy, you not only find perfect alignment with your *Inner Being* and with who-you-really-are, but you also find vibrational alignment with all things that you desire.

When joy is really important to you, you do not allow yourself to focus upon things that do not feel good—and the result of thinking only thoughts that feel good would cause you to create a wonderful life filled with all things that you desire.

When you hold the desire to be joyful and you are sensitive to the way you feel, and therefore guide your thoughts in the direction of things that feel better and better, you improve your vibration, and your *point of attraction* becomes one that will only attract—through the *Law of Attraction*—things that you desire.

Deliberately guiding your thoughts is the key to a joyful life, but a desire to feel joy is the best plan of all . . . because in the reaching for joy, you find the thoughts that attract the wonderful life you desire.

Isn't it Selfish to Want More Joy?

Jerry: Some would say that for a person to want to be joyous all the time would be a very selfish way to want to be, as though desiring joy is a negative.

Abraham: *We are often accused of teaching selfishness, and we always agree that we certainly do teach selfishness, for you cannot perceive life from any perspective other than from that of yourself. Selfishness is the sense of self. It is the picture that you hold of yourself.* Whether you are focusing upon yourself or another, you are doing it all from your selfish vibrational viewpoint, and whatever you are feeling is your *point of attraction.*

So, if from your perspective of self you are focused in a way that you are feeling good, then your *point of attraction* is such that the things that you are attracting—through the *Law of Attraction*—will please you when they get there.

If, however, you are not selfish enough to insist upon focusing in a way that feels good, and you are focused upon something that feels bad, then your *point of attraction* is such that you are negatively attracting—and you will not like what is coming when it gets there.

Unless you are selfish enough to care about how you feel, and there-fore direct your thoughts in such a way that you are allowing a true con-nection to your <u>Inner Being</u>, you have nothing to give another anyway.

Everyone is selfish. It is not possible to be otherwise.

Which Is More Moral, Giving or Receiving?

Jerry: So, you would seem to see as much that is right and joyful in *giving* as in *receiving*. In other words, you don't see one as morally superior to the other?

Abraham: Because of the powerful *Law of Attraction,* whatever you are giving—by way of your vibrational offering—you are receiving. . . . The <u>*Law of Attraction* *always accurately sorts things out*</u> <u>*and brings to everyone the matching product of their thoughts.*</u> So when you give a thought of Well-Being, you always receive the matching equivalent. When you offer thoughts of hatred, the *Law of Attraction* cannot bring you loving results. That defies the *Law.*

Often when people speak of giving and receiving, they are referring to gifts of action, or material things, but <u>the *Law of Attraction* is not responding to your words or actions, but instead to the</u> <u>vibration that is at the basis of those words and actions.</u>   *Sponso-ring thoughts*

Let us say that you see those who are in need of something. Perhaps they have no money, transportation, or food. And as you see them, you feel sad (because you are focused on their lack and activating that within your own vibration), and from your place of sadness you offer them the action of money or food. The vibration that you are transmitting is actually saying to them, *I do this for you because I see that you cannot do this for yourself.* Your vibration is actually focused upon their *lack* of Well-Being and therefore, even though you have offered money or food through your action, *your dominant offering is perpetuating their lack.*

<u>It is our encouragement that you take the time to imagine those</u> <u>people in a better situation.</u> <u>Practice the thought of their success</u> <u>and happiness in your own mind, and once that is the dominant</u> <u>vibration that you hold about them,</u> then offer whatever inspired

action you now feel. In that case, because of the dominant vibration of your Being, as you are holding them as your object of attention, you will attract a matching vibration of Well-Being from them. In other words, you will uplift them. You will assist them in finding the vibration that matches their desire for Well-Being instead of the vibration that matches their current situation. In our view, that is the only kind of *giving* that has value.

So the question is not "Which is superior, giving or receiving?" The question is "Which is superior, focusing upon what is *wanted* or upon what is *unwanted?*" "Which is superior, uplifting another by believing in their success, or adding to their discouragement by noticing where they are?" "Which is superior, being in alignment with my *Inner Being* and then taking action, or being out of alignment and taking action?" "Which is superior, adding to one's success or adding to one's failure?"

The greatest gift that you could ever give another is the gift of your expectation of their success.

There are as many different worlds as there are perceivers, Beings, or individuals. You are not here to create one world where everyone is the same, wanting and getting the same. You are here to be that which you want to be, while you allow all others to be that which *they* want to be.

What If Everyone Got Everything They Wanted?

Jerry: Let me play the part of devil's advocate here. If each of the selfish Beings on the planet were getting everything they individually want, what kind of mess would this world be in?

Abraham: It would not be, and is not, a "mess" at all. For, through the *Law of Attraction*, they would attract unto them those who are in harmony with *their* intent. You see, this is a very well-balanced place in which you live. There is some of everything here, in enough proportion, abundance, and difference, to give you all of the ingredients for this vast and marvelous "kitchen" that you have come to participate in.

How Can I Assist Those Who Are Feeling Pain?

Jerry: I live a joyous and glorious life, but I am often aware that there is much agony being experienced in the world around me. What could I do to make this life experience painless for everyone?

yemen!

Abraham: You cannot create in the experience of another because you cannot think their thoughts. . . . It is the thoughts they are thinking, the words they are speaking, or the acts they are doing that is bringing forth the emotional response (agony) from their *Inner Being. They are creating their own agony by giving thought to that which they do not want.*

?

Now, what you *can* do for them is to set the example of joy. Become a Being who *thinks* only of that which he is wanting; who *speaks* of only that which he is wanting; who *does* only that which he is wanting—and therefore brings forth only joyful emotion.

Jerry: I can do that. I can focus on what I want, on that joy, and I can learn to allow them to have whatever experience they create. So would it be accurate to say that if I focus on their painful experience, that I will now create pain in my own experience? And then I'll be setting *that* example—the example of a painful experience.

Abraham: Let us say that someone in pain comes into your experience and as you see them in their painful situation, a desire wells up inside of you that they find the way out of their painful situation, so their pain only brushed you slightly as you quickly identified your desire for their joyful solution. *If you then turn your undivided attention to their successful resolution of their painful situation, you would feel no real pain, and you could be a catalyst to inspire an actual solution for them. That is an example of what true upliftment is. However, if you only focus upon their pain, or upon the situation that has caused it, you will activate within yourself the vibration that matches that, and you will also begin to feel pain as you then begin the attraction of that which you do not want.*

Is Setting a Joyous Example the Key?

Jerry: Is the key to just continue to seek joy myself? To set that example and allow the others—*really allow them*—to have whatever experience they're choosing (in whatever way they are choosing it) for themselves?

Abraham: You really have no other choice but to allow them to have whatever experience they are attracting, because you cannot think for them or vibrate for them—and therefore you cannot attract for them.

True *Allowing* is maintaining your own balance, your own joy, no matter what they are doing. So the advantage that you offer them is that as you remain in balance, connected to your own *Inner Being,* aligned with the wonderful life-giving resources of the Universe, and you hold them as your object of attention, they benefit. The more you feel good as you hold others as your object of attention, the greater the power of your positive influence.

You will know when you have reached the point of *Allowing* them to be, do, or have whatever they want (or do not want), when, as you are aware that they are doing it, you are not feeling negative emotion about it. *When you are an Allower, you are feeling joy as you are observing the experience of all.*

You have come full circle with your questions in helping us explain the three *Laws* that are so very important.

The *Law of Attraction* is responding to the vibration of your thoughts.

As you deliberately offer your thoughts by choosing thoughts that feel good, you allow your connection to your *Inner Being,* to who-you-really-are. When you are connected to who-you-really-are, anyone you hold as your object of attention benefits. And, of course, in all of that, you feel joy!

In time, you will be so aware of how you feel, and you will become so adept at *deliberately* offering your thoughts, that you will predominantly be in the state of positive attraction. And then (really, *only* then) will you be comfortable in letting others create as they choose. *When you understand that unwanted things cannot assert themselves into your experience, but that everything is invited to you and by you through thought, you never again feel threatened by what others may be choosing to live, even if they are very close by—for they cannot be a part of your experience.*

Can I Think Negative Yet Feel Positive?

Jerry: So how can we give our attention to, or have a thought about, something that's negative and not have a negative emotional response to it?

Abraham: You cannot. And we would not suggest that you try. In other words, to say *never* have negative emotion would be the same as saying, "Do not have a *Guidance System.* Pay no attention to your *Emotional Guidance System.*" And that is the opposite of what we are saying. We want you to be aware of your emotions and then guide your thoughts until you feel relief.

As you are focused upon a little (negative) thought, you will feel a little (unwanted) negative emotion. And if you are sensitive to the way you feel and want to feel better, you will change the thought. It is easy to change it when it is a small thought and a small emotion. It is much harder to change when it is a big thought and therefore a big emotion. The emotion will be proportionate, in intensity, to the amount of thought that you have amassed by the *Law of Attraction.* The longer you stay focused upon what you do not want, the greater and more powerful that thought will become. But if you are sensitive to your emotions and you withdraw your attention from the unwanted subject very quickly, you will begin to feel better, and you will stop the attraction of this unwanted thing.

What Are Some Words to Enhance Being Well-Being?

Jerry: Could you give us some words that we could use to help attract a variety of things, like perfect health . . . ?

AFFIRMATIONS

The Law of Attraction

Abraham: *I want perfect health! I like feeling good. I enjoy my good-feeling body. I have many positive memories of feeling good in my body. I see many people who are clearly in a state of good health, and it is easy to see how much they are enjoying their good-feeling bodies. When I think thoughts like these, I feel good. These thoughts are in harmony with a healthy body.*

Jerry: What about perfect financial prosperity?

Abraham: *I want financial prosperity! There are so many wonderful things that are readily available in this wonderful world, and financial prosperity opens the door to so many of those things. Since the <u>Law of Attraction</u> responds to my thoughts, I have decided to focus predominantly upon the abundance that is possible, understanding that it is only a matter of time before my thoughts of prosperity will be matched by the flow of financial prosperity. Since the <u>Law of Attraction</u> will bring me the object of my attention, I choose abundance.*

Jerry: And great relationships?

Abraham: *I want great relationships. I so enjoy nice, clever, funny, energetic, stimulating people, and I love knowing that this planet is abundant with them. I have met so many interesting people, and I love the discovery of fascinating characteristics in the people I meet. It seems that the more I enjoy people, the more people whom I enjoy come into my experience. I love this time of spectacular co-creation.*

Jerry: What about positive Non-Physical experiences?

Abraham: *I want to attract those who are in harmony with me, physical and Non-Physical. I'm fascinated by the <u>Law of Attraction</u> and am comforted by the knowledge that when I'm feeling good, I can only attract that which feels good. I love understanding that the basis of that which is Non-Physical is pure, positive Energy. I enjoy utilizing my <u>Emotional Guidance System</u> so that I can rendezvous with that Source.*

Jerry: And continual, joyous growth?

Abraham: *I am a growth-seeking Being, and it is exhilarating to remember that expansion is not only natural but inevitable. I love knowing that joy is simply a choice. So, since my expansion is inevitable, I choose to have all of it—in joy.*

Jerry: And that will attract these things?

Abraham: Your *words* will not bring you immediate manifestations of what you are asking for, but the more often you say them, and the better you feel while you are saying them, the purer or less contradicted your vibration will be. And soon your world will be filled with these things you have spoken about. . . . *Words alone do not attract, but when you feel emotion when you speak, that means your vibration is strong—and the <u>Law of Attraction</u> must answer those vibrations.*

What Is the Measure of Our Success?

Jerry: What do you see as success? What would you say is the mark of *success?*

Abraham: The achievement of anything that you desire must be considered success, whether it is a trophy, money, relationships, or things. But if you will let your standard of success be your achievement of joy, everything else will fall easily into place. For in <u>the finding of joy, you are finding vibrational alignment with the resources of the Universe.</u>

You cannot feel joy while you are focusing upon something not wanted, or the lack of something wanted; therefore, while you are feeling joy, you will never be in the state of contradicted vibration. And only the contradiction in your own thoughts and vibration can keep you from the things you desire.

We are amused as we watch the majority spending most of their life seeking a set of rules against which they can measure their life experience, looking outside of self for those who will tell them what is right or wrong, when all along they have within themselves a

Guidance System that is so sophisticated, so intricate, so precise, and so readily available.

By paying attention to this *Emotional Guidance System,* and by reaching for the best-feeling thought that you can find right now from wherever you are, you will allow your broader perspective to help you move in the direction of the things that you truly want.

As you sift through the magnificent contrast of your physical time-space reality, consciously aware of the way you feel, and deliberately guiding your thoughts toward those that feel better and better, in time you begin to see your life through the eyes of your broader *Inner Being.* And as you do so, you feel the satisfaction of being upon the path that you chose from your Non-Physical perspective when you made the decision to come forth into this wonderful body. For, from your Non-Physical vantage point, you understood the eternally evolving nature of your Being and the promise that this Leading Edge contrasting environment held. You understood the nature of your magnificent guidance system and how, with practice, you could see this world as your *Inner Being* sees it. You understood the powerful *Law of Attraction* and the fairness and accuracy with which it responds to the free will of all creators.

By reaching for the best-feeling thought you can find, you reconnect with that perspective, and you will shiver with exhilaration as you reconnect with your purpose, with your zest for life, and with *you!*

PART III

The *Science*
of Deliberate
Creation

The *Science of Deliberate Creation:* Defined

Jerry: Abraham, you have spoken to us of *Deliberate Creation.* Would you discuss the value of that to us and clarify what you mean by *Deliberate Creation?*

Abraham: We have called it the *Science of Deliberate Creation* because we are assuming that you want to create on purpose. But actually, it is more aptly called the *Law of Creation,* for it works whether you are thinking of what you want, or of what you do not want. Whether you are thinking of what you do want, or whether you are thinking of the lack of what you want (the direction of your thought is your choice), the *Law of Creation* goes to work upon whatever you are thinking about.

From your physical perspective, this equation of creation has two important parts: the launching of the thought and the expectation of the thought—the *desire* for the creation and the *allowing* of the creation. From our Non-Physical perspective, we experience both parts of that equation simultaneously, for there is no gap between what we desire and what we fully expect.

1. launching of the thought : desire
2. expectation of the thought

Most humans are unaware of the power of their thoughts, the vibrational nature of their Being, or the powerful *Law of Attraction*, so they look to their *action* to make everything happen. And while we agree that action is an important component in the physical world in which you are focused, it is not through your action that you are creating your physical experience.

When you understand the power of thought and practice your deliberate offering of it, you will discover the powerful leverage (in creating) that only comes from *desiring* and *allowing*. When you prepave, or positively anticipate with your thoughts, the amount of action required is far less, and the action is much more satisfying. If you do not take the time to align your thoughts, far more action is required, without the satisfying results.

Your hospitals are filled to the brim with those who are now taking action to compensate for inappropriate thoughts. They did not create the illness on purpose, but they did create it—through thought and through expectation—and then they went to the hospital to take physical action to compensate. We see many people spending their days exchanging their action for money, because the money is essential to the freedom of life in this society. And yet, in most cases, the action is not action in joy. It is an attempt to compensate for misaligned thought.

You have intended action; that is part of the deliciousness of this physical world in which you live. But you did not intend to do your creating through physical action—you intended to use your body to enjoy that which you have created through your thought.

As you set forth your thought in advance, feeling positive emotion, you have then launched your creation, and when you walk through space and time toward that manifestation in the future, expecting that it will be there . . . then, *from that joyful creation that you have launched into the future, you will be inspired to the action that is action in joy.*

When you are taking action in your now, and it is not action in joy, it is our absolute promise to you that it will not lead to a happy ending. It cannot; it defies the *Law*.

Rather than being so ready to jump into action to get the things that you want, we say *think* them into being; *see* them, *visualize* them, and *expect* them—and *they will be.* And you will be guided, inspired, or led to the perfect action that will bring about the process that will lead you to that which you seek . . . and there is a great difference between that which we have spoken and the way most of the world is going about it.

I Invited It by Giving It Thought

Often, as we begin to impart our knowledge to our physical friends regarding the *Deliberate Creative Process,* we meet with resistance, for there are those who have things in their life experience that they do not want. And as they hear us say, "All things are invited by you," they protest, saying, "Abraham, I wouldn't have invited this because I don't want it!"

So we eagerly offer this information to you to help you understand *how* you are getting what you are getting so that you may be more deliberate in your attracting of it, and so you may *consciously* attract those things that you *do* want—while you may avoid attracting those things that you do *not* want.

We know that you are not inviting, attracting, or creating it—on purpose. But we will say to you that you are the inviter, the attractor, and the creator of it . . . because you are doing it by giving thought to it. By *default,* you are offering your thought, and then the *Laws* that you do not understand are responding to your thought, causing results that you do not understand. And so, that is why we have come forth: to speak to you of the *Universal Laws* so that you may understand *how* you are getting what you are getting, so that you may understand how to gain *deliberate* control of your life.

Most physical Beings are so completely integrated into their physical world that they have very little conscious awareness of their relationship with the Non-Physical world. For example, you want light in your bedroom, so you go to the lamp by your bedside, turn a little switch, and watch the light flood the room. Then you would explain to others, "This switch causes the light." But you understand, without our explaining, that there is much more to the story of where the light comes from. And so it is with all things that you are experiencing in your physical setting. You are explaining only a little bit of what makes things happen. We are here to explain the rest of it to you.

You have emerged into your physical dimension from your broader, Non-Physical perspective with great intent and purpose. You have come forth because you wanted this physical experience very much. This is not the first of such experiences for you. You have had many physical, as well as Non-Physical, life experiences. And you have emerged into this one because you want to add to that continuing evolving Being that you-really-are—that Being that through this body and through these physical senses you may not now know, but that Being, indeed . . . that broader, expansive, growth-seeking, joy-seeking, evolving part of *you*.

My *Inner Being* Is Communicating with Me

We want to help you remember that you are the creator of your experience and that there is such joy in being deliberate about that. We want to help you remember your relationship with the Non-Physical part of you, your *Inner Being*, who is aware of you and involved with you in everything that you do.

You do not remember the details of what you have lived before you came into this physical body, but your *Inner Being* is fully aware of all that you have become, and is continually offering you information to assist you in living in the most joyous way possible, in all moments in time.

As you emerged into this life experience, you did not bring with you the memory of that which you have lived before, for those details would only serve to distract you from the power of your *now*. However, because of your relationship with your *Inner Being*, you do have access to the knowledge of that broader perspective, or *Total You*. *Your broader Non-Physical part of you communicates with you, and has done so from the day you emerged into this physical body. That communication comes in many varieties—but all of you are receiving the basic communication that comes forth, in the form of your emotion.*

Every Emotion Feels Good . . . or Feels Bad

Every emotion that you feel is, without exception, communication from your *Inner Being* letting you know, in the moment, the appropriateness of whatever you are thinking, speaking, or acting. In other words, as you *think* a thought that is not in vibrational harmony with your overall intent, your *Inner Being* will offer you negative emotion. As you *do* or *say* something that is not in vibrational harmony with who-you-are and what you want, your *Inner Being* will offer you negative emotion. And, in like manner, when you are speaking, thinking, or acting in the direction of that which *is* in harmony with your intentions, your *Inner Being* will offer you *positive* emotion.

There are only two emotions: One of them feels good, and the other feels bad. You call them all sorts of different things, depending upon the situation that brought them forth. But as you recognize that this *Guidance System* (which comes forth from within you in the form of emotion) speaks to you from your broader, all-inclusive perspective, you will be able to understand that you have the benefit of all the intentions that you hold here today and all of the intentions that you emerged into this physical body with—and that you have the ability to factor in all of the details of *all* your desires and your beliefs, in order to be able to make the absolute appropriate decisions at every point in time.

I Can Trust My Guidance from Within

Many people have set their own intuitive guidance aside, replacing it with the opinions of parents, teachers, experts, or leaders in a variety of disciplines. But the more you look to others for their guidance, the more removed you become from your own wise counsel. So often as we begin to remind our physical friends of who-they-really-are, helping them to reconnect with the *Guidance System* that is within them, they feel hesitation. They have often become convinced of their unworthiness and of their incorrectness, so they are afraid to move forward, trusting their own guidance or their own conscience, because they believe that there may be someone else who knows more clearly than they do what is appropriate for them.

But we want to help you remember the worthy, powerful Being that you are, and your reason for coming into this time-space reality. We want you to remember your intent to explore the contrast of this wonderful environment, knowing that it would give birth to a continual stream of new intentions; and we want you to remember that who-you-really-are—your *Inner Being,* or *Total You,* or *Source*—is joyous in the expansion that you are about. We want you to remember that you can feel, by the power of your emotions in every moment, whether you are seeing your current situation through the eyes of that broader perspective or whether you are cutting yourself off from that *Source* by choosing thoughts that are of a different nature. In other words, when you feel love, that means that the way you are seeing the object of your attention matches the way the *Inner You* sees it. When you feel hate, you are seeing it without that *Inner Connection.*

You intuitively knew all of this, especially when you were younger, but gradually most of you were worn down by the insistence of those older and self-described "wiser" others who surrounded you as they worked hard to convince you that you could not trust your own impulses.

And so, *most of you physical Beings do not trust yourselves, which is amazing to us, for that which comes forth from within you is all that you may trust.* But instead, you are spending most of your physical lifetimes seeking a set of rules or a group of people (a religious or political group, if you will) who will tell you what is right and wrong. And then you spend the rest of your physical experience trying to hammer your "square peg" into someone else's "round hole," trying to make those *old* rules—usually those that were written thousands of years before your time—fit into this *new* life experience. And, as a result, what we see, for the most part, is your frustration, and at best, your confusion. And, we also have noticed that every year there are many of you who are dying, as you are arguing about whose set of rules is most appropriate. We say to you: *That overall, all-inclusive, never-changing set of rules does not exist—for you are ever-changing, growth-seeking Beings.*

If your house were on fire and the firefighters came with their truck—that marvelous equipment with the big, long hoses and all of the water surging through—and sprayed their hoses into your house and extinguished the flame, you would say, "Indeed, that is most appropriate behavior." But if, on a day when there was no fire, those same firefighters and the same hoses were to enter your house spraying water around, you would say, "Indeed, that is *not* appropriate!"

And so it is with the laws that you are passing relative to one another: *Most of your past laws and rules are not appropriate to that which you are now living. If you had not intended growth, you would not be here in this physical life experience. For you are here as an expanding, ever-changing, growth-seeking Being because you want to add unto that which you understand. And, you want to add unto All-That-Is. . . . If that which was figured out long ago was the ultimate, then there would be no reason for your existence today.*

How Am I Getting What I'm Getting?

At first, our insistence that you are the creator of your own reality is met with a joyful acceptance, because most people long for the control of their own experience. But as you come to understand that everything that is coming to you is being attracted by your own thought *(you get what you think about whether you want it or not),* some of you feel uncomfortable with what seems like the overwhelming task of monitoring thoughts, sorting them out, and offering only those that will yield things that you *do* want.

We do not encourage a monitoring of thoughts, for we agree that would be incredibly time-consuming and cumbersome, but instead we recommend a conscious utilization of your *Emotional Guidance System.*

If you will pay attention to the way that you are feeling, then a monitoring of your thoughts is not so necessary. Whenever you are feeling good, know that you are, in that moment, speaking, thinking, or acting in accordance with your intentions—and know that whenever you are feeling bad, you are not aligned with your intentions. In short, whenever there is negative emotion present within you, you are, in that moment, miscreating, either through your thought, your word, or your action.

And so, the combination of being more deliberate about what you want, more clear about what you intend, <u>and</u> more sensitive to the way you feel is, in essence, what the <u>Deliberate Creative Process</u> is all about.

I Am the Sole Creator of My Experience

The big question that usually comes up at this point of our discussion is, "Abraham, how do I know that what comes forth from within me may be trusted? Isn't there someone greater than I who makes all of the rules and wants me to be or do specific things?" And we say, you are the creator of your experience, and you have emerged forth into this physical body through the power of your desire. You are not here to prove yourself worthy of something else; you are not here because you seek greater salvation on some other plane. You are here because you have a specific purpose in being here. You want to be a *Deliberate Creator,* and you have chosen this physical dimension, where there is time and space, so that you may finely tune your understanding and then see the benefits of whatever you have created in thought by allowing it to come into your physical experience. You are adding to the expansion of the Universe, and *All-That-Is* benefits from your existence, by your exposure to this experience and by your expansion.

All that you do pleases that which you seek to please. There is not a list of things that are right and a list of things that are wrong—there is only that which aligns with your true intent and purpose, and that which does not. You may trust your <u>Guidance</u> that comes forth from within you to help you know when you are in alignment with your state of natural Well-Being.

Magnetically, I Attract Thoughts in Vibrational Harmony

The *Law of Attraction* is responsible for much that is obvious in your life experience. You have coined many phrases because of your partial understanding of this *Law*. You say, "Birds of a feather flock together." You say, "The better it gets, the better it gets; and the worse it gets, the worse it gets." You say, "This day started out bad and ended up much, much worse." But even as you are saying these things, most of you do not truly understand how powerful the *Law of Attraction* really is. People are drawn together because of it. Every circumstance and event is a result of it. . . . Thoughts that are vibrationally similar to one another are drawn magnetically to one another through the powerful *Law of Attraction;* people who feel a certain way are drawn to one another, magnetically, through this *Law;* indeed, the very thoughts that you think are drawn one unto the other until what was once a very small or insignificant and not-so-powerful thought may—because of your focus upon it—grow to be very powerful.

Because of the <u>Law of Attraction</u>, *each of you is like a powerful magnet, attracting unto you more of the way that you feel at any point in time.*

As We're Thinking and Speaking, We're Creating

No other creates in your experience. You are doing it all; you get all of the credit. As you observe your own life experience and the experiences of those around you, we want you to understand that there is not a shred of evidence that is contrary to these powerful *Laws* that we are expressing. As you begin to notice the absolute correlation between what you are thinking and speaking—and what you are getting—your understanding of the *Law of Attraction* will continue and your desire to utilize your *Guidance System* to deliberately direct your thoughts will increase. And, of course, you will have a much greater understanding of the lives of those around you as well. (In fact, it is sometimes easier for you to see it with others.)

Have you noticed that those who speak most of illness have more and more illness? Have you noticed that those who speak of poverty live more of it, while those who speak of prosperity have more of it? As you understand that your thoughts are magnetic and your attention to them causes them to grow in power until eventually the subject of the thought becomes the subject of your experience, your willingness to pay attention to the way you feel will help you more deliberately choose the direction of your thought.

It is easy to see the *Law of Attraction* at work as you are involved in a conversation with another. For example, imagine that your friend is speaking of something she is experiencing and you want to be a good friend, so you are focusing upon her words and listening to the examples she is offering about what is happening to her. As you stay focused there longer, your own examples of similar situations come into your mind. As you then join her in conversation by adding the matching stories of your experience, the thought vibration grows stronger still. Enough attention to these subjects and enough conversations about things you have experienced will bring more of the same kinds of experiences to you. And as more and more thoughts are brought forth related to what you do *not* want, you will eventually find yourself absolutely surrounded by thoughts, words, and experiences that are in the direction of that which you do *not* want. (You and your friend will now have even more unpleasant situations to discuss with one another.)

Now if you had been sensitive to the way you were *feeling* as the conversation first began leaning in the direction of what you do not want, you would have been aware of the sick feeling in the pit of your stomach. You would have recognized your *Guidance,* which is essentially saying, *You are thinking and speaking about that which you do not want.* And the reason for that warning signal, that "warning bell," was the discord between who-you-really-are and what you desire, and what you are focusing upon in this moment. Your emotions indicate your misalignment. Your *Guidance* is alerting you to the fact that while you are thinking and speaking of those unwanted things, you are a magnet attracting circumstances, events, and other Beings unto you, and soon you will have in your experience the essence of the very thing that you have been speaking about that you do *not* want.

In like manner, if you are speaking about that which you *do* want, your thoughts will be drawn more unto *that.* You will draw more people to you who will want to talk about what you *do* want. And all the while that you are speaking of what you *do* want, your

Inner Being will be offering you a positive emotion to let you know that you are in harmony with—and that that which you are attracting to yourself is in vibrational harmony with—the essence of the balance of intentions that you hold.

The Delicate Balance Between *Wanting* and *Allowing*

The *Science of Deliberate Creation* is a delicately balanced *Law;* it has two parts: On the one hand, there is the thought of what you want. On the other hand, there is the expectation or belief—or the allowing into your experience—of what you are creating through your thought.

And so, if you say, "I want a new red car," you have literally, through your thought, set forth the beginning of the creation of that new red car into your experience. And now, the more attention you give to that thought, and the more you are able to purely imagine that red car within your experience, the more excited about it you will become. And the more excited you become, or the more positive emotion that comes forth as you think about your red car, then the faster your red car is coming into your experience. Once you have created it through thought, and once you have felt powerful positive emotion while thinking of it, the car moves rapidly into your experience. It has been created, it now exists, and in order to now have it in your experience, you have only to *allow* it. And you allow it by expecting it, by believing it, and by letting it be.

When you doubt your ability to have the new red car, you stifle your creation. If you say, "I want a new red car," you begin the creation of it, but if then you add, *"but* it is too expensive," you hold yourself apart from your creation. In other words, you have done the first part of the creating by your wanting, but you have now hindered the creation of that which you want by not believing, by not expecting, and by not *allowing*—for in order to bring your creations into your physical experience, both parts of the process are necessary.

Just because you are talking about the subject of your creation does not necessarily mean that you are allowing it. When you think about your new red car and you feel excitement about it, you are allowing it, but when you are thinking about your new red car from a place of worrying that you cannot achieve it (or frustration that it has not yet come), you are actually focused upon the *absence* of the car, and you are not allowing it into your experience.

Sometimes in the early stages of the creation of something you want, you are right on track for receiving it as you are feeling excited about it and are positively expecting it, but then you express your desire to another, who begins to tell you all of the reasons why it *cannot* be, or why it *should not* be. Your friend's negative influence would not be serving you, for when you were focused upon the *essence of your desire*, you were attracting it, but now that you are focused upon the *lack of your desire*, you are pushing what you want away.

How Does It Feel, Good or Bad?

And so, as you say, "I want a new red car, and I know it is coming to me," it is. But as you are saying, *"But where is it? I have wanted it for a very long time. I believed Abraham, but the things that I want are not coming,"* now you are not focused upon what you want. Now you are focused upon the *lack* of what you want, and you are getting, through the *Law of Attraction,* what you are focused upon.

If you focus upon whatever you want, you will attract whatever you want. If you focus upon the lack of whatever you want, you will attract more of the lack. (Every subject is really two subjects: what you want and the lack, or absence, of what you want.) If you are paying attention to the way you are feeling, you will always know whether you are focused upon what you want or upon the lack of it—for when you are thinking of what you want, you are feeling good, and when you are thinking of the lack of what you want, you are feeling bad.

As you say, "I want money to support my lifestyle," you are attracting the money, but as you focus upon the things that you want that you do not have, noticing the lack—you are pushing your abundance away.

An Exercise to Assist in *Deliberate Creation*

Here is an exercise that will assist you in your *Deliberate Creating:*

> *Take three separate pieces of paper, and at the top of each* **1.**
> *page write one thing that you want. Now take the first page, and*
> *beneath the subject of what you have written, write: "These are*
> *the reasons that I want this. . . ." Write whatever comes to your*
> *mind—write whatever flows forth naturally; do not try to force*
> *it. And when nothing more comes, you are complete for now.*
>
> *Now, turn your paper over and write at the top of the second* **2.**
> *side of the page: "These are the reasons that I believe that I will*
> *have this. . . ."*

The first side of your page enhances what you want (the first side of the equation of *Deliberate Creation*). The second side of the page enhances your belief that you will have it (the second side of the equation of *Deliberate Creation*). And now that you have focused upon and activated within your vibration both sides of the equation, you are now in the state of receiving the manifestation of your desire, for you have successfully accomplished both sides of the *Creative Process*. All that is necessary now is that you want it—and continue to expect it until you have it—and it will be yours.

There is no limit to the number of things that you can simultaneously create, for it is not difficult to hold a desire and at the same time hold an expectation of achieving it. But in the beginning, while you are still learning to focus your thoughts, it may be helpful to deliberately concentrate upon only two or three desires at a time, for the longer the list of things you are working on, the greater the potential for doubt to creep in as you look at all the things that you have not yet accomplished. The more you play the game, the better you become at focusing your thoughts, and eventually there will be no reason to limit your list in any way.

Before you can experience something in your physical life experience, you must first give thought to it. Your thought is the invitation, and without it, it will not come. We are encouraging an *intentional* deciding of what is wanted, and then an *intentional* giving of thought to those things that you *want* while you are *intentionally* not giving thought to those things that you do not want. And, in suggesting this, we encourage that you set some time aside every day when you sit and *intentionally* bring your thoughts together into a sort of vision of what you want to experience in your life, and we have been referring to this time as your *Workshop for Deliberate Creating*.

As you are moving through your daily experience, set forth the intention to notice things that you like: *Today, no matter what I'm doing and no matter whom I'm doing it with, it is my dominant intention to look for things that I like.* And as you deliberately gather this data, you will have the available resources to effectively create when you go to your *Creative Workshop*.

Thoughts Evoking Great Emotion Manifest Quickly

We have told you that your thoughts are magnetic. But we want to add a point of clarification here: *Although every thought has creative potential, the thoughts that do not bring great emotion with them are not bringing the subject of your thought into your experience with any sort of speed. When it comes to thoughts that you feel strong emotion about—whether it is positive emotion or negative emotion—the essence of those thoughts is being quickly manifested into your physical experience. And that emotion that you are feeling is communication from your Inner Being, letting you know that you are now accessing the power of the Universe.*

If you go to a horror movie, and as you are sitting there in the theater with a friend, looking at the screen and all of the frightening detail that is being offered with the color and the sound, you are, at that time, in a *negative Workshop*. For as you are envisioning all that you do *not* want to see, the emotion that you are feeling is your *Inner Being* saying to you, *You are seeing something that is so vivid that the Universe is now offering power unto it.*

But when you leave the theater, fortunately, you usually say, "It was only a movie," so you do not *expect* it. You do not *believe* it will happen to you, so you do not complete the second part of the equation. You have given thought to it with emotion, so you have created it, but you do not allow it into your experience because you do not really *expect* it. However, as you are walking out of the theater, if your friend says to you, "It may only be a movie, but it once happened to *me*," then you may begin pondering *that* thought, and in doing so, you may bring yourself to the *belief* or *expectation* that that could also happen to *you*—and then it will. *Giving thought, on the one hand, and expecting or believing, on the other hand, is the balance that brings to you that which you receive.*

If you want it and expect it, it will be yours very soon. However, it is not often that you have achieved a balance where your wanting and your expecting are equal. Sometimes your wanting is very high, but your belief is not there at all. For example, in the story of the mother whose child is trapped beneath the automobile, she does not *believe* that she can lift that heavy vehicle off of her child, but her *wanting* is so extreme that she does. On the other hand, there are many examples where your belief is high, but your wanting is not. The creation of an illness, such as cancer, is that sort of example where your *belief* in it is very keen, while your *wanting* of it is not.

Many of you find yourselves in what we would term a negative *Workshop* many times a day. As you are sitting at your desk with your stack of bills beside you, feeling tension or even fear because there is not enough money to pay them, you are in a negative *Workshop*. For as you sit there giving thought to not having enough money, you are in the perfect position for the creating of more of what you do *not* want. The way you are *feeling* about that is the signal from your *Inner Being* saying to you that what you are thinking is not in harmony with what you want.

A Summary of the *Deliberate Creation Process*

Now let us summarize all that we have offered here so that you may have a clear and definite plan for the deliberate control of your life experience: First, recognize that you are more than you see here in this physical body; and that there is a broader, wiser, certainly older part of you that remembers all that you have lived, and, more important, knows that which you now are. And, from that all-encompassing perspective, this part of you can offer you clear and absolute information as to the appropriateness of that which you are doing, speaking, or thinking, or of that which you are *about* to do or *about* to speak.

Now if you will clearly set forth the intentions that are yours at this time, then your *Guidance System* can work even more effectively, for it has the ability to include all of the data—gathered from *all* of your experiences (all of your desires, all of your intentions, and all of your beliefs)—and compare it with what you are doing, or about to do, in order to give you absolute guidance.

Then, as you are moving through your day, be sensitive to the way you are feeling. And whenever you find yourself feeling negative emotion, stop whatever it is you are doing that is bringing the emotion forth, for the negative emotion means that, in this moment, you are negatively creating. *Negative emotion exists only when you are miscreating. And so, when you recognize that you are feeling negative emotion—no matter why, no matter how it got there, no matter what the situation is—stop doing whatever it is that you are doing and focus your thoughts on something that feels better.*

Practice the *Deliberate Creating Process* for 15 or 20 minutes every day by sitting quietly, undisturbed and undistracted by that which is around you, daydreaming about your life, seeing yourself as you want to be, and envisioning yourself surrounded by that which pleases you.

Attention to *What-Is* Only Creates More *What-Is*

The *Law of Attraction* is responding to *you*, to your *point of attraction*—and your *point of attraction* is caused by your thoughts. The way you *feel* is caused by the thoughts that you are thinking. So the way you *feel* about yourself is your strong and powerful magnetic *point of attraction*. When you *feel* poor, you cannot attract prosperity. When you *feel* fat, you cannot attract thin. When you *feel* lonely, you cannot attract companionship—it defies the *Law*. Many around you want to point out "reality" to you. They say, "Face the facts. Look at *what-is*." And we say to you, if you are able to see only *what-is*—then, by the *Law of Attraction*, you will create only more of *what-is*. . . . You must be able to put your thoughts beyond *what-is* in order to attract something different or something more.

Your emotional attention to *what-is* will root you like a tree to this spot, but an emotional (happy) vision of what you would like to begin attracting into your experience will bring you those changes. *Much of what you are now living, you want to continue, so keep giving your attention to those things, and you will continue to hold those things in your experience. But anything that you do not want, you must take your attention from.*

Appreciation of It Attracts It to Me

Thoughts that evoke your emotions are those that most quickly effect change in your life. Thoughts that you think while feeling no emotion will maintain what is already there. And so, those things that you have already created and appreciate can be kept in your life by continuing to appreciate them. But those things that you do not yet have that you want very soon (and very much), you must give clear, conscious, deliberate, emotion-evoking thought.

An extremely effective use of the *Creative Workshop* is to ponder the aspects you appreciate regarding the subjects that are most important to you. Each time you revisit a subject, your attention to detail will grow stronger, and with more time and more detail, your emotion about the subject will increase, also. Utilizing the *Creative*

Workshop in this way accomplishes everything that is required for *Deliberate Creation,* for you are thinking about something that you want, and in your emotion of appreciation, you are allowing that which you desire to manifest into your experience. As you often go to your *Creative Workshop,* you will begin to notice an obvious correlation between the things you are contemplating inside your *Workshop* and the manifestations that are showing up in your life experience.

Will *Universal Laws* Work Without My Belief?

Jerry: Abraham, tell me, these *Laws* that you speak of, these *Universal Laws,* do they work even if we don't believe that they work?

Abraham: They do, indeed. You are offering vibration even when you do not know you are doing it; that is why there is creating by *default.* You cannot turn your *Creative Mechanism* off; it is always functioning, and the *Laws* are always responding. That is why there is such value in understanding the *Laws.* Not understanding them is a little bit like coming into a game where you do not know the rules. And so, as you are playing the game, you do not understand *why* you are getting what you are getting. And that sort of game becomes frustrating, and most want to leave it.

How Do I Not Get What I Don't Want?

Jerry: Abraham, how would you tell people how to *not* get what they *don't* want?

Abraham: Do not think about what you do not want. Do not give thought to that which you do not want—for your attention to it attracts it. The more you think about it, the more powerful your thought becomes, and the more emotion comes forth. However, when you say, "I'm not going to think about that subject anymore," in that moment you are still thinking about that subject. So the key is to think about something else—something that you *do* want. With practice you will be able to tell by the way you feel if you are thinking about something wanted or unwanted.

This Civilized Society Seems Short on Joy

Jerry: We live in what I call a very civilized society, and in economical and material aspects we are doing relatively well, yet I don't see much joy in the people around me on the streets and in the businesses, and so on and so forth. Is that because of those factors that you speak about . . . that they have very little desire but a strong belief?

Abraham: Most people offer the majority of their vibration in response to what they are observing. And so, when they observe something that makes them feel good, they feel joy, but when they observe something that makes them feel bad, they simply do not feel joy. And most people do not believe that they have any control over the way they feel because they cannot manage to gain control over the conditions to which they are having these feeling responses. It is their belief in the lack of control of their own experience that is most responsible for the absence of joy that you are noticing. And we must remind you that if you continue to notice their lack of joy—yours will be gone as well.

I Want to Want with More Passion

Jerry: You've also said that if our *wanting* is passionate, our *belief* doesn't need to be so strong. So how would we go about building a passionate desire into the *Workshop* that you speak of?

Abraham: There must be a beginning place for all things. In other words, many who are interacting with us say, "Abraham, I hear what you're saying, but I don't know what I want." And so we say, begin by stating: *I want to know what I want.* For in setting forth that statement, you will become a magnet that will attract all sorts of data from which you can make your decisions. *Begin somewhere, and let the Law of Attraction deliver unto you examples and choices; and then the more you think about those choices, the more passionate you will be.*

Attention to any subject will cause it to grow stronger, and the emotion will therefore increase as well. When you think about what you want and you continue to add details to the picture, those thoughts grow stronger. But when you think about something that you desire but then think about it not yet coming . . . and then you think about how much fun it will be to have it, but then remember that it costs a great deal of money and you cannot yet afford it . . . that back-and-forth thinking dilutes your passion and slows the power of your thoughts.

Could I Release Counterproductive Beliefs?

Jerry: Could people create in one particular desired direction even though they've been led to believe (by others) that they're *destined* to create in a different direction?

Abraham: If their wanting is enough, they could. In other words, the mother we mentioned in the story earlier was taught by her society and by her own life experience to believe that she could not pick up an automobile that weighed so much, yet when her wanting was keen enough (when her child was in jeopardy), she was able to do it. And so, if the wanting is great enough, beliefs can be overridden.

Beliefs are very powerful, and they are slow to change, but they *can* be changed. As you continue to reach for better and better-feeling thoughts, you will find them and activate them, and the *Law of Attraction* will respond to them, and in time, your new life will reflect those changes in thought. If you hold to the idea that you can only believe the things that are currently based in "factual evidence," then nothing can change for you, but when you understand that the refocusing of thought, and the response of the

Law of Attraction to the new thought, will bring new evidence, then you understand the power of *Deliberate Creation*.

Can Past-Life Beliefs Affect My Current Life?

Jerry: Are there any thoughts (or beliefs) from any of our past lives that are still creating, or capable of creating, circumstances in our current physical experience?

Abraham: You are a continually expanding Being, and your *Inner Being* is the culmination of all that you have lived. Your *Inner Being* not only believes, but knows, the worthiness and value of your Being, so as you choose thoughts that are in agreement with those of your *Inner Being*, you feel the clarity of that knowledge.

However, the details of any past physical experience do not affect you in this physical experience. There is much confusion about that, and it comes largely because there are those who do not want to accept that they are the creator of their own experience. They say, "I'm fat in this life experience because I starved to death in the last." And we say: *There is nothing from past-life experience that is influencing that which you are doing now, unless, in some way, you have become aware of it and are now giving it your attention.*

Can My Negative Expectations
Affect the Well-Being of Others?

Jerry: If, in our concern for the welfare of those we really care about, we find our thoughts drifting toward some negative expectation regarding them, can we, just by pondering a problem occurring in *their* lives, actually cause them damage?

Abraham: *You cannot create in the experience of another because you cannot offer their vibration—which is their point of attraction—for them.* But when you focus upon something long enough that your thought becomes strong, and you are feeling strong emotion about it, you can *influence* the thoughts that they are thinking about a subject.

Remember, most people offer most of their vibration in response to what they are observing, so if they are observing you and see that look of concern on your face, or are observing the concerned comments you are making, they may very well lean in the direction of what is not wanted.

If you want to be of greatest value to others, see them as you know they want to be. That is the influence that you want to offer.

Can I Undo Past Programming by Others?

Jerry: If one's mind has been "programmed" by others into some belief, and this person finds that this belief is no longer desirable in their life, how can this person undo those beliefs?

Abraham: *You are negatively influenced by two major hindrances: One is the influence of others; the other is the influence of your own old habits. . . .* You have developed patterns of thinking, so you can easily fall into those old habitual patterns rather than think the new thought that is in harmony with the new desire. It is a matter of deliberately utilizing a little strength, or as you say, willpower, and refocusing your attention in a new direction.

The "programming" that you are referring to is only the result of your having focused upon something and then upon *Law of Attraction*'s response to that focus, so anything that you focus upon will grow stronger. Some of what you may be calling "programming" is merely a healthy integration into your current society, but some of it actually hinders your personal expansion. In time, and with practice, you will be able to tell the difference, and guide your thoughts in the direction of *your* personal choices. And that is really what *Deliberate Creation* is all about.

My Point of Power Is Right Now?

Jerry: Abraham, there's a phrase from the *Seth* books that says: *Your point of power is in the present.* What does that mean to you?

Abraham: Whether you are thinking about something that is occurring right now or about something that has happened in your past, or about something that you would like to occur in your future—you are doing the thinking right now. You are offering your vibration of thought in your present, and it is this present-thought vibration that the *Law of Attraction* is always responding to; therefore, your power to create is *now.*

It is also helpful to acknowledge that your emotion is coming forth in response to your *current* thought, whether it concerns your *past, present,* or *future.* The greater the emotion you are feeling, the more powerful your thought is, and the faster you are attracting into your experience things that match the essence of that thought.

You could be recalling an argument you had with someone many years earlier, or with someone who may have died ten years ago, but as you are recalling the argument *now,* you are activating the vibration of it *now,* and your current *point of attraction* is being affected by it *now.*

How Did the First Negative Thing Occur?

Jerry: I've often wondered how the first disease, or the first negative thing, occurred. Is it true that the first of almost everything occurred through the thought of it? In other words, like the first electric light, the thought came first and then the electric light followed, so our advancement into more diseases or into good or exciting things is only one step, or one thought, beyond something that has been previously thought?

Abraham: *All things—whether you determine that they are good or bad—are just the next logical steps from where you are currently standing.*

You are correct when you understand that the thought comes first. First there is thought, then thought-form, then manifestation. Your current situation is a platform of experience that inspires the next thought and the next.

When you realize that you can choose to positively expect, or negatively expect, but in either case, the *Law of Attraction* will add power to the thought until it will eventually manifest, you may wish to become more deliberate in the direction of your thoughts. Nothing ever manifests from your first, subtle attention to it. It takes time and attention to a subject to draw enough power to it to cause its manifestation. That is why all kinds of things, both wanted and unwanted, increase. In other words, diseases increase and become more plentiful as humans focus more and more upon diseases.

Is Imagination Not the Same as Visualization?

Jerry: Abraham, how would you describe the term *imagination?* What does it mean to you?

Abraham: *Imagination* is the mixing and massaging of thoughts into various combinations. It is similar to observing a situation. However, in imagination, you are creating the images rather than watching something in your current reality. Some use the word *visualization,* but we want to offer this subtle distinction: *Visualization* is often only a memory of something that you have once observed. By *imagination,* we mean deliberately bringing desired components together in your mind to create a desired scenario. In other words, focusing with the intention of inducing positive emotion. When we use the term *imagination,* we are really talking about *Deliberately Creating* your own reality.

Jerry: But how could a person visualize or imagine something that they haven't seen yet, like a mate they would like to have, a child they would like to give birth to, or a vocation that they've never considered?

Abraham: As you observe the world around you, deliberately gather and ponder the aspects of life that are appealing to you. Notice the beautiful smile that someone offers you or the beautiful home that someone lives in. Make mental or written notes about the things you enjoy in your world, and then mix those components together in your own mind, creating scenarios and versions of life that please you. Do not look for perfect role models, for you are unique and the creator of your own unique reality.

In time, you will discover, or remember, that this art of imagination will cause pleasing results to make their way into your experience, but the art of imagination is also very entertaining and fun. As you begin saying, "I want to know what I want," you will begin to attract, by *Law*, all sorts of examples. And as you are collecting the data that comes to you, let your dominant intent, in each day, be to look for things that you want. Then you can look around you and see in others those traits or characteristics that you would like to have in your own mate or companion or work. *Truly, the perfect role model for you, regarding any subject, does not exist—you are the creator of that.*

Sometimes we hear it said, "I wanted to be wealthy, and then I met a man who was wealthy, but he had bad health and a rotten marriage, so then I associated prosperity with rotten marriages and bad health, so I no longer wanted prosperity." And we say, collect the prosperity data if you want it—and leave out the bad health and the bad marriage.

Jerry: So we can visualize piecing together all of the desired characteristics of the mate or the child or the work that we've wanted?

Abraham: Yes. And that is really the point of the *Workshop*. It is a place where you can go, undistracted, and where you begin to formulate pictures in your mind.

Jerry: So it doesn't have to be something that's already existed, ever; it has to be just what you now feel you want to experience?

Abraham: And as you are working in your *Workshop,* you will find that, in most cases, it will not come to you instantly. You will know when you are clear because you will feel excited. . . . Have you ever been working on a project and you thought about it, you thought about it quite a lot, and suddenly you say, "I have a good idea!"? That feeling of *I have a good idea!* is your point of launching your creation. In other words, you have been mulling the thoughts over in your mind until you have become specific enough that when you hit upon the perfect combination of thoughts, your *Inner Being* offered you emotion saying, *Yes, that is it! Now you have it!* And so, the point of the *Workshop* is to think about all sorts of things until you feel that sensation of a good idea.

Jerry: When a strong intention that we've been visualizing hasn't yet materialized, what's the most common cause for that?

Abraham: *If you have been <u>purely</u> visualizing your intention, then it must come, and come quickly.* The purity of the visualization is the key, and by that we mean purely offering thoughts only in the direction of what you want. When you say, "I want it, *but* . . ." as you add your *but,* you cancel it or defeat it at birth. Often you are offering as many or more thoughts about the absence of your desire as you are about the presence of your desire. *If something you want is slow to come to you, it can be for only one reason: You are spending more time focused upon its absence than you are about its presence.*

If you could identify what you want and then *deliberately* think clearly upon what you want until you get it, the essence of all things that you want would be yours very quickly. If you could spend your time purely envisioning what you want, rather than giving your attention to the reality of *what-is,* you would be attracting more of what you want instead of more of *what-is.* It is a matter of changing your magnetic *point of attraction.*

Get your eyes, words, and thoughts off of <u>what-is,</u> and put them purely on what you now want. The more you think and speak of what you want, the faster what you want will be yours.

Is Being Patient Not a Positive Virtue?

Jerry: Abraham, how do you feel about telling someone, "Just be patient"?

Abraham: When you understand the *Law of Attraction,* and when you begin to deliberately direct your own thoughts, the things you desire will flow quickly and steadily into your experience—and patience will not be necessary.

We are not excited about anyone learning patience, for it implies that things naturally take a long time, and that is not true. They only take a long time in coming when your thoughts are contradicted. If you move forward then backward, then forward then backward, you could potentially never get to where you want to go. But when you stop moving backward and only move forward, you will get there quickly. And that does not require patience.

I Want to Take a Quantum Leap

Jerry: Well, it's easy to take a small step beyond where we are and just *do* a little more than what we've been doing, *be* a little more of what we are, and *have* slightly more than what we now have, but how about what we call a "quantum leap"? In other words, achieving something almost beyond anything that we've ever seen before. How would one go about creating something like that?

Abraham: Good. Now you have hit upon the key. The reason it is easier for you to take those small steps forward is because it is easy for you to acknowledge the beliefs that you now hold and stretch those beliefs just a little bit. You are not completely changing your beliefs; you are just expanding them a little bit. "Quantum leap" often means you must release your current belief and adopt a new one.

Quantum leaps are not achieved by enhancing the belief part or the allowing part of the equation. Quantum leaps are achieved by enhancing the wanting part.

Would you not agree that the mother who (in the story we offered) lifted the automobile from her child experienced a "quantum leap"? If she had been in a gymnasium, it would have taken a very long time, little by little, to convince herself she could pick up something that heavy. But her powerful desire caused the "quantum leap" in the moment.

We are not proponents of "quantum leaps" because they require exaggerated contrast, which causes a dramatic propulsion of your desire and can produce a startling result. But that result is almost always temporary, for the balance of your beliefs will eventually bring you back to where you were before. A gradual bridging of beliefs in the direction of your desires is a much more satisfying way to create.

Jerry: And tell me one more time: How can we fan our desire? How can we make ourselves want more?

Abraham: Put your thoughts upon what you believe you want, and the *Law of Attraction* will draw more information, more data, and more circumstances to your creation.

You see, it is a natural process that when you look at what you want, you will feel powerful, positive emotion. So it is a matter of holding your thoughts upon what you want. If possible, go to the places where the things that you want are so that you deliberately put yourself in that position of feeling wonderful. And as you are feeling good, all things that (by your estimation) are good will begin coming into your experience.

When you focus upon something, the *Law of Attraction* will do the "fanning." So if it seems that it is requiring a great deal of work for your desires to increase and the positive emotion to be more, it is because you are thinking about what you want and then about its opposite, so you are not allowing steady, forward motion.

Aren't the Grander Things Harder to Manifest?

Jerry: Then what would you say is the reason why almost everyone feels that they can create or manifest little things, but they feel like they can't create the larger things?

Abraham: It is because they are not understanding the *Law*, and they are hinging what-can-be upon what-has-been. . . . *When you understand the <u>Laws</u>, then you understand that it is not more difficult to create a castle than it is a button. They are equal. It is not more difficult to create $10 million than $100,000. It is the same application of the same <u>Law</u> to two different intentions.*

Can I Prove These Principles to Others?

Jerry: When a person wants to test these *Laws* or principles in order to try to prove their validity to someone else and they're saying, "Let me show you what I can do with this," does that have any bearing on the effectiveness of the *Law of Attraction?*

Abraham: The problem with trying to prove something is that it often causes you to push against something that you do *not* want. And as you do that, you activate *that very thing* in your vibration, which makes it more difficult to accomplish what you *do* want. It also can be discouraging, for if *they* have strong doubt, they may influence *you* to have some doubt.

There is not a need to prove anything to anyone with your words. Let that which you are—that which you are living—be your clear example to uplift others.

Why Is There a Need to Justify One's Worthiness?

Jerry: Abraham, why do you feel that so many of us, in physical form, seem to have a need to justify the good that comes to us?

Abraham: Part of the reason is that humans incorrectly believe in the limitation of resources, so they feel they must explain to others why they should receive it instead of *them*. Belief in "unworthiness" is another factor. There is a very powerful thought here in your physical dimension that says, "You are not worthy, so you are here to *prove* yourselves as worthy."

You are not here to prove your worthiness. *You are worthy!* You are here for the experience of joyful expansion. It was by the power of your desire, and by the power of your allowing—indeed, by your application of the very *Laws* that we are discussing here—that you have emerged into this time-space reality. And so, your physical existence here is proof of your worthiness, or deservedness, to be, do, or have whatever you desire, you see.

If you could realize that the reason your thought about your "unworthiness" feels so bad is because that thought is in utter disagreement with the way your *Inner Being* feels, you might then seek to improve the direction of your thought. But if you do not understand that, then often you flounder around, trying to please others, but because there is no consistency in what they ask of you, eventually you lose your way.

When you are in the mode of justifying, you are in a negative mode, for you are not focused upon what you want. Instead, you are trying to convince others that it is all right for you to desire, and you need not do this. It *is* all right.

How Does *Action,* or *Work,* Fit into Abraham's Recipe?

Jerry: So many of those I've seen who've had tremendous results in their life—people to whom joyous things happen materially, with relationships, and healthwise—don't seem to put out very much physical energy to receive these things. They seem to work a lot less than a lot of the other folks who seem to work much harder but who then receive so much less. So where does the *physical work,* or *action* part, fit into your recipe for creating what we want?

Abraham: You did not come into this environment to create through *action*. Instead, your *action* is meant to be a way in which you enjoy what you have created through *thought*. When you take the time to deliberately offer your thought, discovering the power of aligning the thoughts of your desires with matching beliefs and expectations, the *Law of Attraction* will yield to you the results you are seeking. However, if you do not take the time to line up your thoughts, there is not enough *action* in the world to compensate for that misalignment.

Action that is inspired from aligned thought is joyful action. Action that is offered from a place of contradicted thought is hard work that is not satisfying and does not yield good results. When you really feel like jumping into action, that is a clear sign that your vibration is pure and you are not offering contradictory thoughts to your own desire. When you are having a hard time making yourself do something, or when the action you offer does not produce the results you are seeking, it is always because you are offering thoughts in opposition to your desire.

You are mostly physical-action Beings at this time because you do not yet understand the power of your thought. When you are better at applying your deliberate thought, there will not be so much action for you to tend to.

I Am Prepaving My Future Circumstances

Often people will say to us, "Well, Abraham, I have to offer action—I can't just sit around and think today." And we agree that your lives are under way, and that they do require action. But if we were standing in your physical shoes, we would, today, begin to offer as much deliberate thought about the things that are important to us as we could. And when we found ourselves thinking about things we do not want (thoughts which are always accompanied by negative emotion), we would stop and make an effort to find a better-feeling way of thinking about that. And in time, things would begin to improve on all subjects.

Let us say that you are walking down a street and you find a big bully (by your estimation) beating up a smaller person. Some sort of action is required right now! Your options, at this stage of this manifestation, are either to walk away and let the smaller person be hurt, or to get involved and perhaps risk getting hurt yourself. Neither option is satisfying.

So, take whichever action you choose, but do not leave your thought where it is right now. Gather positive images from life experience of people living more harmoniously, and take *them* to your *Workshop,* and make *those* kinds of thoughts the most active vibrations within you. And, in time, the *Law of Attraction* will not bring you into situations where there seem to be no positive choices.

*One who sees himself as a "savior," saving little ones from the big ones, will find himself often coming across people who need to be saved. . . . And if it is your desire to have these kinds of experiences, then continue the thought of those kinds of experiences—and the Law of Attraction will continue to bring them to you. But if you pre-*fer something different, think about that—and the *Law of Attraction* will bring *that* to you. *The subjects of your thoughts are prepaving your future experiences.*

How the Universe Fulfills Our Diverse Desires

Jerry: I used to tell people that my observation had been that those who worked the hardest through life had the least, and those who worked the least had the most. And yet, somebody had to dig the potatoes, milk the cows, drill the holes for the oil, and do what we call the *hard work.* So explain to me, Abraham, how can it all work out so that each of us can still have, do, and be what we want, no matter what kind of work needs to be done.

Abraham: You are living in what we see as a perfectly balanced Universe. You are like chefs in a well-stocked kitchen, and all of the ingredients that have ever been imagined are here in abundant proportion to allow you to create whatever sort of recipe you want. When you really *do not* want to do a thing, it is hard for you to imagine that there are others who may *want* to do it, or who do not mind doing it.

It is our absolute knowing that if your society decided that they did not want to do a certain task, by the power of your wanting, you would come forth with another way of doing it, or of doing without it. It is a common thing for a society to reach the point where there is no longer a desire for a thing, and so it ceases to be, while it is replaced with a new and improved intention.

How Does Physical Life Differ from the Non-Physical?

Jerry: What are the chief differences in *our* life, here in our physical experience, and *your* life, in your Non-Physical dimension? What do *we* have here on Earth that *you* don't have?

Abraham: Since you are a physical extension of that which we are, much of what you experience, we do as well. We do not allow ourselves, however, to focus upon the things that bring *you* discomfort. We are more keenly focused upon what *is* wanted, and therefore we do not experience the negative emotion that you experience.

You have the ability to feel as we feel, and in fact, when you are in the mode of *appreciation*, for example, or *love*, the very emotion that you feel is your indication that you are looking at your current situation in the same way that we see it.

There is no separation between what you know as the physical world and what you see as our Non-Physical world; however, in the Non-Physical world, our thoughts are purer. We do not push against what is not wanted. We do not think about the lack of what is wanted. *We give our undivided attention to continually evolving desires.*

Your physical world, Earth, is a nice environment for fine-tuning your knowledge, for here your thoughts do not translate into an instant equivalent—you have a buffer of time. As you set forth your thoughts of what you want, you must become very clear (clear enough that emotion comes forth) before you begin the attracting process. And even then, you must *allow* it and *expect* it into your experience before it manifests. That *buffer of time* provides you with much opportunity to be very clear about how desirable the thought *feels* to you.

  buffer of time

If you were in a dimension where you were instantly manifesting, you would be spending more of your time trying to get rid of your mistakes (as many of you are now doing anyway) than you would in creating the things you want.

What Prevents Every Unwanted Thought from Manifesting?

Jerry: What is it—in that *buffer of time* zone—that culls out the unwanted from our thoughts before they physically manifest?

Abraham: In most cases, it is not "culled" out. Most people have a little bit of the things they like, and a little bit of the things they don't like. *Most are creating almost everything in their lives by default because they do not understand the rules of the game. They do not yet understand the <u>Laws.</u>*

But there are those who are coming to understand these *Eternal Universal Laws* (and by that we mean that they exist even in your ignorance of them, and they exist in all dimensions). For those people, then, their awareness of the way they are *feeling* is what makes the difference as to which of their thoughts manifest.

Shouldn't I Visualize the Means of Manifestations?

Jerry: Abraham, when we're visualizing or thinking about something that we want, should we be looking at the *means* (or the *how*) of obtaining it as well as *whatever* we want to obtain? Or would it be smarter to just visualize the final result only, and let the *how,* more or less, take care of itself?

Abraham: If you have already identified that you want to participate in the specific *means,* then it is all right to give your attention to that.

The simple key to knowing whether you are not specific enough or too specific is by the way you *feel.* In other words, as you are in your *Workshop,* the specifics of your thought will bring forth the enthusiasm, or the positive emotion; but if you become too specific before you've collected enough data, then you will feel doubtful or worried. *And so, recognizing the balance of your intentions is a matter of paying attention to the way you feel. . . . Be specific enough that you feel positive emotion, but not so specific that you begin feeling negative emotion.*

When you speak of _what_ you want and _why_ you want it, you usually feel better. However, when you speak of _what_ you want and _how_ it will come to you, if you do not right now see a way that it will unfold, then that specific thought will feel worse. If you speak of _who_ will help it to come, _when_ it will come, or _where_ it will come from, and you don't have any of those answers, then those specifics are hindering more than they are helping. _It really is a matter of being as specific as you can be, while still continuing to feel good._

Am I Too Specific in My Desires?

Jerry: Let's say that I'd like to be a teacher in a very joyous situation. Would it be any advantage to say, "Well, then, I should decide whether I want to teach history, math, or philosophy, or whether I want to teach high school or something else"?

Abraham: As you think about the *reason* that you want to be a teacher: *I want to uplift others to the joy that I have discovered in this specific knowledge,* your positive emotion indicates that your thought is helping your creation. But then if you were to think, *But I'm not well versed in this subject* or *There is no freedom for students in this current school system* or *I remember how stifled I felt as a student* or *I never had a teacher I liked,* these thoughts do not feel good, and the *specifics* of them are hindering your joyful creation.

The question is not about whether you should be specific or general. The question is about the direction of the thought. What you are reaching for are good-feeling thoughts. So reach for good-feeling thoughts, and realize that you will usually find them faster as you stay general in your approach; but then from that place of feeling good, continue to gently add more and more good-feeling specifics to them until you can easily be very specific and feel good at the same time. This is the best way to create.

Jerry: Would we be better off to just envision the essence of the end result and let the specific details take care of themselves completely?

Abraham: That is a good way of going about it. Fast-forward to the happy end results that you are seeking. Imagine already having achieved whatever it is that you desire. And from that place of feeling good, you will attract the specific thoughts, people, circumstances, and events to bring all of that about.

Jerry: Then how detailed would you recommend our thoughts be about the end result of what we want?

Abraham: *Be as detailed in your thoughts about your desire as you can be—and still feel good.*

Can I Erase Any Disadvantageous Past Thoughts?

Jerry: Is there any way a person could erase the slate of all past experiences, thoughts, and beliefs that aren't of any advantage to our joyous creating in this moment?

Abraham: You cannot look at an unwanted experience and announce that you will no longer think about *that,* because even in that moment you *are* thinking about *that.* But you can think about something else. And in giving your attention to something else, that unwanted subject from your past will lose power and, in time, you will no longer think about it, at all. *Rather than trying so hard to erase the past, focus on the present. Give thought to what you now want.*

How Could One Reverse a Downward Spiral?

Jerry: If you were to find yourself in a downward spiral where all the things that were important to you seemed to be falling away or depreciating, how could you stop the negative downward motion and turn it in a positive upward direction?

Abraham: It is an excellent question. That "downward spiral" is the *Law of Attraction* at work. In other words, it started with a little negative thought. Then more thoughts were drawn unto it, more people were drawn unto it, more conversation was drawn unto it, until it became a very powerful, as you say, downward spiral. It takes a very strong Being to take your thought from what is not wanted when it is that intense. In other words, when your toe is really throbbing, it is difficult to put your thought upon a healthy foot. *In extremely negative situations, we would suggest distraction rather than trying to change the thought. In other words, go to sleep or go to a movie; listen to music; pet your cat . . . do something that will change your thought.*

Even when you are in what you are calling "a downward spiral," some things in your life are better than others. As you focus on the best of what you have, even if it is a small part of what is happening, the *Law of Attraction* will now bring you more of that. *You can replace a fast-moving "downward spiral" with a fast-moving "upward spiral" just by directing your thoughts to more and more things that you do want.*

competition

How about When Two Compete for the Same Trophy?

Jerry: Since, in a competitive situation, when one person *wins* the trophy it means that the other person *loses* it, how can each person get what they want?

Abraham: By recognizing that there are unlimited "trophies." When you *put* yourself in a competition where there *is* only one trophy, you are putting yourself automatically in a situation of knowing that only one will win the trophy. The one who is clearest, the one with the strongest desire and the greatest expectancy of winning, will win it. . . .

Competition can serve you because it stimulates your desire, but it can be a disadvantage if it hampers your belief in succeeding. Find a way to have fun in the competition. Look for the advantages it brings you, even if you do not bring home the trophy. And as you feel good, no matter what, you win what we consider to be the greatest trophy of all. You win *Connection*. You win clarity. You win vitality. You win alignment with your *Inner Being*. And in that attitude, you will bring home more trophies.

In this unlimited Universe, there need be no <u>competition</u> for resources, for the resources are unlimited. You may deprive yourself of receiving them, and therefore <u>perceive</u> a shortage, but it is really of your own making.

If I Can Imagine It, It's Realistic

Jerry: Is there anything that we might want that you would consider to be unrealistic?

Abraham: *If you are able to imagine it, it is not "unrealistic." If, from this time-space reality, you have been able to create the desire, this time-space reality has the resources to fulfill it. All that is required is your vibrational alignment with your desire.*

Jerry: Well, if I can *envision* it in any way, does that mean that I have *imagined* it?

Abraham: As you are *envisioning* yourself within that which you are *imagining*, you are attracting the circumstances whereby you will find the means to create it.

Could We Use These Principles for "Evil"?

Jerry: Could a person use the same process of creation that you're teaching to create what some would see as "evil," like taking the lives of others, or taking things from others, against their will?

Abraham: Is it possible for someone to create what *they* want, even though *you* do not want them to want it?

Jerry: Yes.

Abraham: Indeed. For whatever *they* want . . . they may attract. Hitler, Donald Trump

Is There More Power in Group Co-creating?

Jerry: Can we compound our power, or our ability to create something, by coming together as a group of people?

Abraham: The *advantage* to coming together to create something is that you may stimulate and enhance the desire. The *disadvantage* is that as there are more of you, it becomes more difficult to stay focused only upon what is wanted by you. . . . *Individually, you hold enough power to create anything that you can imagine. Therefore, you do not need to come together with others. It can, however, be fun!*

What If They Don't Want Me to Succeed?

Jerry: Is it possible to create effectively when we're in the company of people who strongly oppose what we want?

Abraham: By focusing upon what *you* desire, you could ignore their opposition. If you oppose their opposition, however, then you would not be focused upon what you want, and your creation would be affected. It is easier to walk away where you no longer need to focus on the opposition in order to stay focused upon your desire. But if you need to walk away from someone because of the potential for opposition, then you need to get out of town, too, for most certainly there are those there who are not in total agreement with your ideas; and out of this country; and off of the face of this planet. *Removing yourself from opposition is not necessary. Just focus upon what you want, and by the power of your own clarity, you will be able to positively create under any circumstances.*

Jerry: Are you saying that we will be receiving the essence of everything we are thinking about—whether it's something we do want or something we don't want—as long as it has emotion connected to it?

Abraham: If you are thinking a thought and you remain focused upon it long enough, the *Law of Attraction* will deliver more thoughts unto it until it becomes clear enough that emotion will be evoked. *Every thought that you think, if you keep thinking it, will eventually become powerful enough to attract the essence of itself into your experience.*

How Do I Use My Momentum's Flow for Growth?

Jerry: Abraham, how can we get into a state of flow where the momentum that we've created is now adding to our growth—that is, to our forward motion?

Abraham: By finding one small thing that makes you happy when you think about it, and then focusing upon it until the *Law of Attraction* brings more and more and more. The more you think of what you want, the more positive emotion will come forth . . . and the more positive emotion that comes forth, the more you will know that you are thinking about what you want. And so, it is a matter of you—deliberately and consciously—making the decision of which direction of flow you want.

Everyone, without exception, is attracting everything that comes into their experience, but when you deliberately choose the direction of your thought, gently guiding your attention to better-feeling thoughts, you will no longer create unwanted things by default. Your conscious awareness of the powerful *Law of Attraction,* coupled with your determination to pay attention to your emotions and your desire to feel good, will cause you to experience the joy of *Deliberate Creation.*

PART IV

The Art of Allowing

The *Art of Allowing:* Defined

Jerry: Abraham, this next subject, I would say, has had the most impact in the way of new understanding for me because I'd never thought of it from the perspective and with the clarity that you have, and that's the *Art of Allowing.* Would you speak about it?

Abraham: We are most eager to help you remember your role in the *Art of Allowing* because a deliberate understanding and application of this *Law* brings everything together for you. In other words, the *Law of Attraction* just *is,* whether you understand that it is or not. It is always responding to you and giving you accurate results, which always match what you are thinking about. But a deliberate application of the *Art of Allowing* requires that you be consciously aware of the way you feel so that you choose the direction of your thoughts. An understanding of this *Law* is what determines whether you create *intentionally* or by *default.*

We have put the *Art of Allowing* in this order, following the *Law of Attraction,* first; and the *Science of Deliberate Creation,* second, because the *Art of Allowing* cannot begin to be understood until the first two are.

What we mean by the *Art of Allowing* is: *I am that which I am, and I am pleased with it, joyful in it. And you are that which you are, and while it is different perhaps from that which I am, it is also good. . . . Because I am able to focus upon that which I want, even if there are those differences between us that are dramatic, I do not suffer negative emotion because I am wise enough not to focus upon that which brings me discomfort. I have come to understand, as I am one who is applying the Art of Allowing, that I have not come forth into this physical world to get everyone to follow the "truth" that I think is the truth. I have not come forth to encourage conformity or sameness—for I am wise enough to understand that in sameness, in conformity, there is not the diversity that stimulates creativity. In focusing upon bringing about conformity, I am pointed toward an ending rather than to a continuing of creation.*

And so, the *Art of Allowing* is absolutely essential to the continuation or the survival of this species, of this planet, and of this Universe, and that continuation is powerfully allowed from the broader perspective of Source. You, from your physical perspective, may not be allowing your own expansion, and when you do not, you feel rotten. And when you do not *allow* another, you feel rotten.

When you see a situation that bothers you and you decide that you will do nothing to try to stop it or change it, you are *tolerating* the situation. That is very different from what we mean by *allowing*. *Allowing* is the art of finding a way of looking at things that still allows your connection to your *Inner Being* at the same time. It is achieved by selectively sifting through the data of your time-space reality and focusing upon things that feel good. It is about using your *Emotional Guidance System* to help you determine the direction of your thoughts.

Shouldn't I Protect Myself from Others' Thoughts?

Jerry: The question that was difficult for me in the beginning of this was: How do we protect ourselves from others who are thinking differently from us, differently enough that they might invade our space, so to speak, in some way?

Abraham: Good. That is why we said that before you can understand and accept the *Art of Allowing,* you must first understand the *Law of Attraction* and the *Science of Deliberate Creation.* For, certainly, if you do not understand how something is coming unto you, then you are fearful of it. If you do not understand that others cannot come into your experience unless you invite them through thought, then of course you would worry about what others are doing. But when you understand that nothing will come into your experience unless you invite it through your thought—with emotional thought and great expectation—then unless you actually accomplish this delicate creative balance, you will not receive it.

When you understand these powerful *Universal Laws,* you no longer feel a need for walls, barricades, armies, wars, or jails; for you understand that you are free to create your world as you want it to be, while others are creating their world as they choose it to be, and their choices don't threaten you. You cannot enjoy your absolute freedom without this knowledge.

In this physical world, there are those things that you are in absolute *harmony* with, and there are those things that you are in absolute *disharmony* with—and there is some of everything in between. But you have not come forth to destroy or contain that which you do not agree with, for that is a continually changing thing. Instead, you have come forth to identify, moment by moment, segment by segment, day by day, and year by year, what it is *you* want, and to use the power of your thought to focus upon it and to allow the power of the *Law of Attraction* to draw it unto you.

We Are Not Vulnerable to the Behaviors of Others

The reason most are not willing to allow what some others are doing is because, in their lack of understanding of the *Law of Attraction,* they incorrectly believe that the unwanted experience can seep or jump into their experience. As they live unwanted experiences, or see others doing so, they assume that since no one would deliberately choose these bad experiences, the threat must be real. They fear that if others are allowed to behave in that way, it will spread into their own experience. In their lack of understanding of the *Law of Attraction,* they feel defensive and vulnerable, so walls are constructed, and armies are assembled from this place of vulnerability, but to no avail. For pushing against these unwanted things only produces more of them.

We are not offering these words so that you may free your world from all of its contrast, for the very contrast you would like to eliminate is responsible for the expansion of *All-That-Is.* We offer these words because we understand that it is possible for you to live joyful lives amidst the enormous variety that exists. These words are being offered to assist you in finding the personal freedom that you will experience only when you understand and apply the *Laws of the Universe.*

Until the first two *Laws* are understood and applied, the *Art of Allowing* cannot be understood or applied, for it is not possible for you to be willing to *allow* others until you understand that what they do and what they say need not affect you. Because your feeling—one that comes from the very core of your Being—is so very powerful that, because you want to preserve your own self, you cannot and will not *allow* one who threatens that.

These Laws that we are presenting to you are Eternal, which means that they are forever. These Laws are Universal, which means that they are everywhere. They are Absolute, whether you know that they are or not; they exist, whether you accept that they exist or not—and they influence your life, whether you know that they do or not.

The Rules of the Game of Life

When we use the word *Law,* we are not referring to the Earthly agreements that many of you term *law.* You have the law of gravity, and you have the law of time and space, and you have many laws, even laws regarding the controlling of your traffic and the behavior of your citizens. But when *we* use the word *Law,* we are speaking of those everlasting, ever-present *Universal Laws.* And there are not as many of them as you might believe there are.

If you will come to understand and apply these three basic *Laws,* you will have an understanding of how your Universe functions.

You will have an understanding of how everything that comes into your experience comes. You will recognize that you are the inviter, the creator, and the attractor of all things that come to you; and you will, indeed, then have deliberate control of your own life experience. And, in all of that, you will then, and only then, feel free—for freedom comes from an understanding of *how* you get *what* you get.

Here, we will express the rules of your game of physical experience, and we do so enthusiastically, because they are the same rules of the game of all life, whether it is physical life experience or Non-Physical life experience.

The most powerful *Law* in the *Universe*—the *Law of Attraction*— simply says that that which is like unto itself is drawn. You may have noticed that when bad things begin to happen in your life, it seems that everything starts to go wrong. But when you wake up in the morning feeling good, you have a happier day. However, when you begin the day with a fight with someone, you find that the rest of your day is negative in many regards—that is your awareness of the *Law of Attraction*. And, indeed, everything that you are experiencing—from the most obvious to the most subtle—is influenced by this powerful *Law*. . . . When you think about something that pleases you, by the *Law of Attraction*, other thoughts that are similar to it will begin to come forth. When you think of something that displeases you, by the *Law of Attraction*, other thoughts that are like that will begin to come forth until you find yourself reaching into your past for similar thoughts; and you will find yourself discussing them with others until you are surrounded by a larger and larger, ever-growing larger, thought. And as this thought is growing larger and larger, it is gaining momentum; it is gaining power . . . attraction power. An understanding of this *Law* will put you in a position where you may decide to focus your thoughts *only* in the direction of what you *want* to attract into your experience, while you may decide to take your attention from those thoughts that you do not want to draw into your experience.

Now, the *Law of Deliberate Creation* is described in this way: *That which I give thought to, I begin to attract. That which I give thought to that brings forth strong emotion, I attract more quickly. And once I have launched it powerfully by giving thought that evokes emotion, then, as I expect that which I have thought about—I get it.*

The balance of *Deliberate Creation* is two-sided, so to speak. On the one hand is the thought, and on the other hand is the expectancy or the belief, or the *Allowing*. And so, when you have given thought to something and are now expecting it or believing that it will be, now you are in the perfect position to receive the subject of your thought. That is why you get what you think about, whether you want it or not. Your thoughts are powerful, attractive magnets—attracting one to another. *Thoughts attract to themselves, and you attract thoughts by giving your attention to them.*

It is usually easier to see these *Laws* at work when you look into others' experiences: You will notice that those who speak most of prosperity, have it. Those who speak most of health, have it. Those who speak most of sickness, have it. Those who speak most of poverty, have it. It is *Law*. It can be no other way. *The way you feel is your point of attraction, and so, the Law of Attraction is most understood when you see yourself as a magnet, getting more and more of the way you feel.* When you *feel* lonely, you attract more loneliness. When you *feel* poor, you attract more poverty. When you *feel* sick, you attract more sickness. When you *feel* unhappy, you attract more unhappiness. When you *feel* healthy and vital and alive and prosperous—you attract more of all of those things.

Life Experiences, Not Words, Bring about Our Knowing

We are teachers, and in all of our experiences of teaching, we have learned this most important fact: *Words do not teach. It is life experience that brings you your knowing.* And so, we encourage you to reflect into your own life experience to remember those things that you have experienced before, and to begin watching, from this point forward, for the absolute correlation between the words that you are reading here in this book and the life experience that you are living. And so, when you begin to notice that you are getting what you are thinking about, then, and only then, will you want to pay attention to (in fact, to deliberately control) your thoughts.

Controlling your thoughts will become easier when you make the decision that you will do it. You think about things you do not want, mostly because you have not understood how detrimental it is to your experience. For those of you who *do not* want those negative experiences, and for those of you who *do* want those positive experiences, *once you have recognized that thinking of what you do not want only attracts more of what you do not want into your experience, controlling your thoughts will not be a difficult thing, because your desire to do so will be very strong.*

Rather Than Monitor Thoughts, I'll Feel Feelings

Monitoring your thoughts is not an easy thing to do, for while you are monitoring your thoughts, you are not having time to think them. And so, rather than monitoring your thoughts, we are going to offer to you an alternative, an effective alternative. There are very few who understand that while you are a physical Being, focused through this physical apparatus, that simultaneously there is a part of you—a broader, wiser, and certainly an older part of you—that exists at the same time, and that part of you (we refer to it as your *Inner Being*) communicates with you. The communication takes many different forms. It may come in the form of clear, vivid thought—even an audible spoken word at times—but in all cases, it comes to you in the form of emotion.

You set forth, before you emerged, an agreement that communication with your Inner Being would exist. And it was agreed that it would be a feeling, one that could not be missed, rather than a stimulation of thought or an offering of words that could be missed. For, as you are thinking your thoughts, you might not always receive a different thought that is being offered in that same moment. Just as when you are thinking, or deep in thought, you sometimes do not hear what someone who is standing in the same room with you is saying to you. And so, the process of feeling, as in emotion, is a very good process for communication.

There are two emotions: One feels good and one feels bad. And it was agreed that the feeling that feels good would be offered when you are thinking, speaking, or doing that which is in harmony with what you want; while it was agreed that a feeling that feels bad would be offered when you are speaking, thinking, or acting in a direction that is not in harmony with your intentions. So, it is not necessary for you to monitor your thoughts. Simply be sensitive to the way you are feeling, and anytime you feel negative emotion, recognize that you are—in the moment of that feeling—miscreating. In the moment of that negative feeling, you are thinking a thought of something you do not want, thereby attracting the essence of it into your experience. Creation is the process of attraction; when you think a thought, you attract the subject of your thought.

When I'm Tolerating Others, I'm Not *Allowing*

And so, this essay has been prepared that you might understand that there is not another who is, or offers, any threat to you. For you are the controller of your own experience. The *Art of Allowing*, which says, *I am that which I am, and I am willing to allow all others to be that which they are,* is the *Law* that will lead you to total freedom—freedom from any experience that you do not want, and freedom from any negative response to any experience that you do not approve of.

When we say it is good to be an *Allower,* many of you misunderstand what we mean by that, for you think that *Allowing* means that you will *tolerate.* You will be that which you are (which by your standards is that which is appropriate), and you will let everyone else be that which they want to be, even if you do not like it. You will feel negative about it; you will feel sorry for them; you may even feel fearful for yourself, but, nevertheless, you will let them be—but in a tolerant fashion.

When you are *tolerating,* you are not *Allowing.* They are two different things. One who *tolerates* is feeling negative emotion. One who is an *Allower* does not feel negative emotion. And that is a very great difference, for it is the absence of negative emotion that is freedom, you see. You cannot experience freedom when you have negative emotion.

Tolerance may seem to be an advantage for others because you are not hindering them from what they want to do. But tolerance is not an advantage to *you,* because while you are being tolerant, you are still feeling negative emotion, and therefore, you are still negatively attracting. Once you become an *Allower,* you will no longer attract into your experience those unwanted things, and you will experience absolute freedom and joy.

Am I Seeking Solutions or Observing Problems?

Many would say, "Abraham, do you mean that I should put my head in the sand? I should not look and see those who are having trouble? I should not look for an opportunity where I may be of assistance to them?" And we say, if you intend to be of assistance, your eye is not upon the *trouble* but upon the *assistance,* and that is quite different. *When you are looking for a solution, you are feeling positive emotion—but when you are looking at a problem, you are feeling negative emotion.*

You can be of great assistance to others as you see what they want to be, and as you uplift them to what they want to have, through your words and through your attention to that. But, as you see one who is down on his luck, as you see one who has great poverty or great illness, and as you speak with him in pity and sympathy about that which he does not want, you will feel the negative emotion of it, because you are a contributor to that. As you talk to others about what you know they do not want, you assist them in their miscreating, because you amplify the vibration of attracting what is not wanted.

If you see friends who are experiencing illness, try to imagine them well. Notice that when you focus upon their illness, you feel bad; but when you focus upon their possible recovery, you feel good. By focusing upon their Well-Being, you *allow* your connection to your *Inner Being,* who also sees them well, and you may then influence your friend to improvement. When you are in connection with your *Inner Being,* your power of influence is much greater. Of course, your friends may still choose to focus more upon the illness than the wellness, and in doing so, may remain sick. If you let your friends influence you to thoughts that cause negative emotion within you, then their influence toward the unwanted is now stronger than your influence toward the wanted.

I Uplift Through My Example of Well-Being

You will not uplift others through your words of sorrow. You will not uplift others through your recognition that what they have is not what they want. You will uplift them by being something different yourself. You will uplift them through the power and clarity of your own personal example. As you are healthy, you may stimulate their desire for health. As you are prosperous, you may stimulate their desire for prosperity. Let your example uplift them. Let what is in your heart uplift them. You will uplift others when your thought feels good to you. . . . You will depress others, or add unto their negative creating, when your thought makes you feel bad. That is how you know whether or not you are uplifting.

You will know that you have achieved the state of *Allowing* when you are willing to allow another, even in their not allowing of you; when you are able to be that which you are, even when the others do not approve of what you are; when yet you are able to still be that which you are, and not feel negative emotion toward their thoughts about you. When you can look into this world and feel joy all of the time, you are an *Allower.* When you are able to know which experiences contain joy and which ones do not—and you have the discipline to participate only where there is joy—you will have achieved *Allowing.*

The Subtle Difference Between *Wanting* and *Needing*

Just as the difference between positive emotion and negative emotion can sometimes be very subtle—*the difference between wanting and needing can be very subtle.*

When you are focusing upon what you *want,* your *Inner Being* offers you positive emotion. When you are focusing upon what you *need,* your *Inner Being* offers you negative emotion because you are not focused upon what you want. You are focused upon the *lack* of what you want—and your *Inner Being* knows that that which you give thought to is that which you attract. Your *Inner Being* knows that you do not want the lack; your *Inner Being* knows you want what you want, and your *Inner Being* is offering you guidance so that you will know the difference.

Focusing upon a <u>solution</u> makes you feel positive emotion. Focusing upon a <u>problem</u> makes you feel negative emotion, and while the differences are subtle, they are very important, for when you are feeling positive emotion, you are attracting into your experience that which you want. When you are feeling negative emotion, you are attracting into your experience that which you do not want.

{ wanting
  allowing
  receiving

I Can Create Deliberately, Intentionally, and Joyfully

So, we might say, an *Allower* is one who has learned the *Law of Deliberate Creation* and has reached the position where he does not miscreate. He creates deliberately, intentionally, and joyfully. You see, *contentment* comes from only one place. Contentment comes only from wanting, then allowing, and then receiving. And so, as you are moving through this experience of physical life, holding your thoughts in the direction of what is wanted, letting the powerful *Law of Attraction* work for you, bringing more and more of the events and circumstances and other Beings who are compatible with you into your experience—then you will find your life spiraling upward to joy and freedom.

You have some questions for us regarding the *Art of Allowing?*

I Am Living the *Art of Allowing*

Jerry: I do have questions, Abraham. To me, the *Art of Allowing* is the most exciting topic of them all.

Abraham: *Allowing* is that which you have come forth into this experience to teach. But before you can teach, you must know.

Ordinarily, this subject comes up more in the line of, "Someone is doing something I do not like; how can I get them to do something I do like instead?" And what you will come to understand is: *Rather than trying to get the world to all do the same thing, or to do the things that you like, it is a much better plan to put yourself in the position of accepting that everyone has the right to be, do, or have whatever they want; and that you, through the power of your thoughts, will attract unto you only that which is in harmony with you.*

How Can I Know Right from Wrong?

Jerry: I didn't know about the *Art of Allowing* before meeting you, so the way I used to decide what was right or wrong for me was, if I was considering some particular action, I'd try to imagine what the whole world would be like if everyone did it. And then if it looked like it would be really a joyous or comfortable world, then I'd go ahead with the action. And if it looked like a world that I wouldn't want to live in if *everybody* was doing it, then I'd decline to perform the action, so to speak.

I'll give you an example. I used to like to stream-fish for trout, and at first I fished like everyone else did. I caught every fish that I could possibly catch. But I guess I became a little uncomfortable regarding the rightness or wrongness of doing that, and I thought, *What would it be like if the whole world did that?* And in my imagination, I realized that if everyone caught fish the way I did, we'd fish all these streams empty and there wouldn't be any fish left for others to have this spectacular pleasure that I was having. So with that, then my new decision was that I wouldn't *kill* any of the fish. I would catch them (on barbless lures), but I would turn them loose. In other words, I'd use a lure without a barb on it, and I'd only take the fish out of the water that someone had asked me to bring back for them to eat.

Abraham: Good. *That which any of us has to offer of greatest value is the example of that which we are. Our words can add to that example, our thoughts can add to that example, and certainly, our actions add* to that example. But the key for any of us—in our desire to uplift this world—is to make more clear decisions about what we want to be at any point in time—and then to be that.

That which you were doing, in your example, is in harmony with that which we are teaching now, in that once you decided what you wanted, then your *Inner Being* offered you emotion to help you know the appropriateness of what you were about to do. In other words, once you had decided that you wanted to uplift this world, once you had decided that you wanted to add unto it and not take from it disproportionately, then any action that you began to make, or that you anticipated making, that was not in harmony with that intention would have felt uncomfortable to you.

You had exaggerated your desire for the world to be a better place by imagining that everyone in the world did whatever it was you were thinking about doing—which brought forth exaggerated guidance from within. It is a good way of going about it. You were not trying to get them all to do it; you were only using that *idea* of them all doing it to help you be clear about whether it was a good thing for *you* to do or not. And it was a good plan.

But What about When I Observe Others Committing Wrongs?

Jerry: It worked for me, so my fishing days were ones of absolute, spectacular joy. But I still felt uncomfortable when I saw other people wasting fish and killing them just for the fun of it . . . or whatever their reason.

Abraham: Good. Now we have come upon a very important point. As *your* actions were in harmony with *your* intentions, you felt joy. But as *others'* actions were not in harmony with *your* intentions, you did not feel joy. And so, what is required is that you set forth another set of intentions regarding the others. A very good set of intentions regarding others is this: *They are that which they are, creators of their own life experience, attracting unto themselves, while I am creator of my experience, attracting unto me. That is the Art*

What about the fish?

of Allowing. . . . And as you state that to yourself again and again, soon you will come to recognize that they are not really messing up your world in the way that you might think that they are. They are creating their own world. And to them, it may not be a world that is messed up.

What is difficult is when you are looking at your world as one that is not abundant . . . when you begin thinking in terms of how many fish there are, or when you begin thinking in terms of how much prosperity and abundance is present. For then you begin to worry about someone else wasting it or squandering it, leaving not enough for the rest, or not enough for you.

When you come to understand that this Universe . . . indeed, this physical experience in which you are participating, is abundant—and that there is not an ending to that abundance—then you do not worry. You let them create and attract to *them,* while you create and attract to *you.*

Will Ignoring the *Unwanted* Allow the *Wanted?*

Jerry: Well, the way I resolved that dilemma, in essence, was that back in 1970, and for the following nine years, I completely turned off my input from what I'll call the outside world. I turned off my television and my radio, I didn't read newspapers anymore, and I also turned off a lot of people who were talking about things I didn't want to hear. Again, that decision worked for me. It worked so well that during that nine-year period I achieved what I felt were magnificent results in the areas of the meaningful relationships that evolved with many other people, the regaining and maintaining of perfect physical health, and the development of significant financial resources. It was fulfilling, like nothing that had happened before in my life. But by my shutting out that negative input in that way and keeping my attention upon my intentions, it was really more like just sticking my head in the sand than it was what you're calling *Allowing.*

Abraham: There is great value to giving your attention to what is important to you. As you put your head in the sand, so to speak, closing out much of the outside influences, you were able to focus upon that which was important to you. As you give thought to anything, you draw power, clarity, and results to it, you see. And as you do that, you receive contentment—the contentment that comes only from wanting, allowing, and achieving.

As far as being one who was ignoring, or putting your head in the sand, not paying attention, rather than being an *Allower*, perhaps those fit together better than you think. . . . *Giving your attention to what is important to you is the process by which you will allow others to be that which they want to be. To give your attention to yourself, while you allow them to give their own attention to themselves, is a very important process in the art of becoming an Allower.*

Jerry: In other words, because I was expecting (although I'd never heard the words before) the *Law of Attraction* and the *Deliberate Creation Process* to work for me, I had automatically shifted into the stage of *Allowing*, in a sense of the word?

Abraham: That is correct. You were giving your attention to what was important to you, therefore attracting more of that, which made watching television not interesting and reading newspapers not important. *It was not that you were depriving yourself of something that you wanted; instead, by the Law of Attraction, you were drawn more to what you most wanted.* As you observe things on the television or in the newspaper that, because you do not want them, make you feel negative emotion—you hinder your allowance of what you *do* want.

Do We All Want to Allow Joyousness?

Jerry: Are most of us, in physical form, seeking to understand this *Art of Allowing*? Or are you saying that only those of us who are speaking to you want that understanding?

Abraham: All of you who exist upon Earth today, in physical bodies, intended, before your emergence into these bodies, to understand and be an *Allower*. But most of you, from your physical perspective, are far from understanding it or wanting it; you would rather try to *control* one another than *allow* one another. It is not difficult to learn to control the direction of your thoughts, but it is utterly impossible to control one another.

But What about When Others Are Having Negative Experiences?

Jerry: So, is this state of *Allowing* that we are, from some level, seeking, one in which we can still see and be aware of the negatives around us (or what feels negative from our perspective) and still remain joyous? Or will we not be able to see it at all? Or, won't we see it as negative?

Abraham: All of that. When you were focused upon the things that were important to you, you were not watching the television and you were not reading the newspapers—you were enjoying what you were doing. You were giving your attention to what was important to you, and the *Law of Attraction* brought more and more and more and more power and clarity to that. And so, the other was simply not drawn into your experience because it did not fit with your intentions of growth and achievement.

When you are clear about what you want, you do not have to force-fully keep yourself upon the track, for, by the Law of Attraction, it occurs. And so, it is not difficult to be an Allower. It comes easily and simply because you will not be so interested in all of those things that have nothing to do with what you are about.

Your television, while it offers you much information that is of value, offers much, much more information that has very little to do with what any of you want in your life experience. Many of you sit and watch the television simply because it is there, because no other decision has been made, and so watching the television is not so much, usually, a *deliberate* act as it is an action by *default*. And in that state of not-deliberateness, in that state of no-decision, you are opening yourself to being influenced by whatever is thrown at you. And so, as you are being bombarded, literally, with the stimulation of thoughts of unwanted things that occur all around your world, and because you have made no decision about what you *do want* to think about, you find yourself accepting into your experience, through thought, many things that you would not have chosen.

This is what creating by default is: giving thought to something without being deliberate about it . . . thinking about it, and thereby attracting it—whether you want it or not.

I'll Only Look for What I Want

Jerry: Abraham, how would you tell me to achieve and maintain this state of *Allowing* that I want, in spite of the fact that I'm aware that there are many around me who, from their perspective, are experiencing pain, or what I call *negatives?*

Abraham: *We would suggest to you that you make a decision—a decision that no matter what you are doing in this day, no matter who you are interacting with, no matter where you are, that your dominant intent will be to look for those things that you want to see. And as that is your dominant intent, by the <u>Law of Attraction</u>, you will attract only those things that you want to attract, and you will see only those things that you want to see.*

A *Selective Sifter* as a Selective Attractor

As your dominant intent is to attract only that which you desire, you will become a more *selective sifter.* You will become a more selective attractor. You will become a more selective noticer. In the beginning, you will still notice that you are attracting some of that which is not to your liking because you will have set forth some momentum from thoughts and beliefs that have been before this time. But, in time, once Well-Being has been your dominant intention at the beginning of every day for 30 to 60 days, you will begin to notice that there is very little that is in your life experience that is not to your liking—for your momentum, your thought, will have carried you beyond what is now occurring.

It is difficult to be an *Allower* when you see someone very close to you doing that which you feel threatens you, or doing that which threatens someone else. And so, you say, "Abraham, I don't understand what you mean when you say I can think it away, that through my thoughts I can deal with it, and that no action need be taken." And we say, it is through your thoughts that you invite, but what you are living today is a result of thoughts that you have thought before this time, just as the thoughts that you are thinking today, you are projecting into your future. Your thoughts today are now prepaving your future, and there will be a point in time when you will move to *that* future place, and you will *then* live the results of the thoughts that you are thinking *now*, just as today you are living the results of the thoughts that you have thought before.

Our Past, Present, and Future as One

You are always thinking, and you cannot disconnect your past, present, and future, for they are all one; they're all tied together with the continuum of thought. And so, let us say you are walking down the street and you come across a fight—there is a very big bully beating up on a much smaller man—and as you walk closer, you are filled with negative emotion. When you think, *I'm going to turn my eyes away; I'm going to walk away and pretend like this has not happened,* you feel terrible negative emotion because you do not want this little one to be hurt. And so, then you think, *Well, I will go in and I will help.* But now you also feel negative emotion because you do not want your own face to be broken or your own life to be taken away. And so you say, "Abraham, now what do I do?" And we say, we agree. In this example, there is not an option that seems to be the perfect one—because you are, in this moment, having to do so much work because of your lack of prepaving in your past.

If, in your past, as you began each day, you had intended safety, you had intended harmony, and you had intended interacting with those who were in harmony with your intentions, it is our absolute promise to you that you would not now be in this uncomfortable position. And so, we say deal with it now in whatever way you choose, but today if you will begin to set forth your thoughts of what you want in the future, you will not find yourself walking into another sort of uncomfortable ambush where no matter which way you go it is not comfortable.

climate change
Trump

Must I Allow the Injustices I Witness?

Until you understand *how* it is you get what you get, it is going to be very difficult for you to accept the idea of *Allowing*, because there are so many things that you see in this world that you do not like, and you say, "How can I allow this injustice?" And we say, you allow it by recognizing that it is not part of your experience. And that, in most cases, it is truly not any of your business. It is not your work. It is the creation; it is the attraction; it is the experience of the others.

Rather than trying to control the experiences of all others (which you cannot do no matter how hard you try), instead, intend to control your own participation within those experiences. And by setting forth your clear image of the life you want to live, you will prepave a smooth and pleasant path for yourself.

My Attention to *Unwanted* Creates More of *Unwanted*

You attract through your thought. You get what you think about, whether you want it or not. And so, as you give attention to the drivers who are not courteous, you will attract more of them into your experience. As you give your attention to those who are not giving you good service as you are going from business to business, you will begin attracting more of those sorts of experiences unto you. *That which you give your attention to—particularly your emotional attention to—is that which you draw into your experience.*

Does the *Art of Allowing* Affect My Health?

Jerry: Abraham, I would like to cover a series of, what I call, everyday, real-life experiences, and have you, if you would, tell me a little bit about how you see the *Art of Allowing* applying to these particular conditions. First, as far as physical health is concerned, I recall having had many years of an extreme physical illness during my childhood. And then I reached a stage in my life when I wanted out of that, so I've had extremely good physical health, in essence, ever since then. How does the *Art of Allowing* fit into those two situations, from extreme illness to extreme health?

Abraham: When you have made a decision about something you want, you have accomplished one-half of the equation for the *Deliberate Creation* of it. You have given thought with emotion, which is what *wanting* is. On the other side of the equation for the *Deliberate Creation* is the *Allowing*, or the expecting, the letting it be. . . . And so, when you say *I want, and I allow, therefore it is,* you will be very fast in your creation of whatever it is that you want. You are literally *allowing* yourself to have it by not resisting it, by not pushing it away with other thoughts.

You have heard us say that when you are in the state of *Allowing,* you do not have negative emotion. The state of *Allowing* is freedom from negativity; therefore, when you have set forth your deliberate intent to have something and you are feeling only positive emotion about it, then you are in the state of *Allowing* it to be. And then you will have it, you see.

To have health instead of illness, you must think about health. When your body is sick, it is easier to notice the sickness, so it requires desire, focus, and a willingness to look beyond what is happening right now. By imagining a healthier body in the future, or by remembering a time when you were healthier, your thought, in the moment, will match your desire, and you will *then* be allowing an improvement in your condition. The key is to reach for thoughts that feel better.

Allowing, from Extreme Poverty to Financial Well-Being

Jerry: The next subject I would like to discuss would be the area of wealth and prosperity. During my childhood, I lived at the poverty end of it, like living in chicken houses and tents and caves, and so on and so forth. And then, in 1965 I found the book *Think and Grow Rich!*, which gave me a different perspective of how to look at things, and from that day forward, my financial life spiraled upward. From living in my Volkswagen bus, I moved on to creating six-figure, and then seven-figure, annual incomes.

Abraham: What do you think took place in that changing of your perspective from the reading of that book?

Jerry: Well, what I remember the most is, I began, for the first time in my adult life, to focus only on what I wanted, more or less exclusively. But I'd like to hear your perspective on that phenomenon.

Abraham: You achieved an understanding that you *could* have what you wanted. The desire was already in place from the living of life, but in reading that book you came to *believe* that it was possible. The book caused you to begin to *allow* your desire to be realized.

Allowing, Relationships, and the Art of Selfishness

Jerry: Another area, a big one that I'd like to talk about, is the area of relationships. There were times when I found it difficult for me to allow friends to have their own thoughts and beliefs, and their own "inappropriate" activities.

Abraham: When you are using the word *allow* in this sense, what do you mean?

Jerry: I felt as if they should *think* and *act* the way I wanted them to think and act. And when they didn't, it made me extremely, and often angrily, uncomfortable.

Abraham: And so, as you were observing what they were doing or what they were speaking, you felt negative emotion—your signal that you were not in the state of *Allowing.*

Is the Art of Selfishness Not Immoral?

Jerry: And I, at that time, thought of myself as very selfless and very giving. In other words, I would not have been considered a selfish person, so I expected them to be less selfish and more giving, also. And the fact that they weren't was very disturbing to me. Then I found David Seabury's book *The Art of Selfishness,* and that made me look at *selfishness* from another perspective, so I was able to understand a lot of my negativity because of that new perspective.

Abraham: It is important that you allow yourself to pay attention to what you want. And there are those who call that *selfishness,* and they do so in a judging or disapproving way. And we say to you that unless you have a healthy view of self, unless you are allowing yourself to want, and expecting to receive that which you want, you will never be deliberate in your creating, and you will never have a very satisfying experience.

The not allowing of self is usually where the not allowing of others comes forth. Usually the one who is most disapproving of a quality in himself notices that same quality in others, and disapproves of it there as well. And so, an accepting, an approving, an appreciating, and an allowing of oneself is the first step in the appreciating, approving, or allowing of others. And that does not mean that you must wait until you are, by your standards, perfect, or that they are, by their standards, perfect, for there will never be that perfect ending place—for you are all ever-changing, ever-growing Beings. It means looking and intending to see in you what you want to see, or intending to see in others what you want to see.

We are often accused of teaching *selfishness,* and we agree that we do. Everything that you perceive is from the perspective of *self;* and if you are not selfish enough to insist on your connection or alignment with your broader, wiser *Inner Being,* then you have nothing to offer to others. By being selfish enough to care how you feel, you can then utilize your *Guidance System* to align with the powerful Energy of *Source,* and then anyone who is fortunate enough to be *your* object of attention, benefits.

Their Disapproval of Me Is Their Lack

If there are others who see something in you that they do not approve of, most often you see their disapproval reflected back through their eyes, and you feel that you have gone wrong in some way. And we say unto you, it is not *your* lack, it is *theirs.* It is *their* inability to be the *Allower* that brings forth their negative emotion; it is not *your* imperfection. And, in like fashion, when you feel negative emotion because you have seen something in others that you do not want to see, it is not *their* lack, it is *your own.*

And so, when you make the decision that you want to see only that which pleases you, then you will begin to see only that which pleases you, and all of your experiences will bring forth positive emotion, because, by the *Law of Attraction,* you will attract unto you only that which is in harmony with what you want. By understanding the power of your emotions, you can then direct your thoughts, and then you will no longer need others to behave differently in order for you to feel good.

But What about When One Is Violating Another's Rights?

Jerry: Here's another area that's given me much discomfort in the past, and that is regarding the rights of one or another: property rights, territorial rights, or rights to our own peace. In other words, I used to be extremely disturbed when a person's rights were violated by violence on a person, or by someone forcefully taking someone else's property. Also, I was torn over territorial rights, and who should be allowed into our country and who should not be allowed into our country. Why should one person be allowed in and another person not? But then, after meeting you, I got to the point that I see all those things they're doing with each other as "games" that they're playing—more or less "agreements" that they have between one another, spoken or unspoken. I've gotten somewhat better at not feeling their pain. But can I get to the point that I don't feel anything negative when I see someone violating the rights of another? Can I just look at whatever they're doing to one another out there, and think, *You're all doing to one another what you have somehow chosen to do?*

Abraham: You can. As you understand that they are each attracting through their thought, then you will be exuberant rather than feeling pain for them, for you will understand that they are reaping the negative or positive emotion, depending upon their choice of thoughts. Of course, most of them do not understand how they are getting what they are getting. And that is the reason why there are so many who believe that they are victims. They believe that they are victims because they do not understand how they get what they get. They do not understand that they invite through their thought or through their attention. It may help you

to realize that each experience causes a clarification of desire.

There Is Not a Shortage of Anything

Now you have mentioned *territorial rights*. We have a rather different view of "territory" than those of you who are in physical form, because in your physical world you continue to see limitation. You feel that there is only so much space, which will eventually all be taken up, so you feel that there is not enough.

In your attitude of limitedness; in your feeling of lack rather than abundance; in your notice of not enough space or not enough money or not enough health, you feel a reason to guard. From our perspective, there is not a limitation of anything, but an ever-flowing abundance of all subjects. There is enough of everything for all of you. And so, as you come to understand that, then any feeling of limitation, of lack, of a need for protection, or of defending territorial rights will not be an issue.

By the *Law of Attraction* we are drawn together. Here in our Non-Physical perspective, this "Family of Abraham" is together because we are, in essence, the same—and in our sameness we are attracted to one another. And so, there is not a keeper of the gate. There are not guards to keep the unharmonious out, for they are not drawn to us because we are not giving our attention to them. It is the same in your environment. While you do not see it as clearly as we do, the *Laws* are working as perfectly for you as they are for us. It is that you have so many physical explanations for things, physical explanations that may be right, in part, but are not the complete explanation. In other words, as you describe how the water gets into your glass by pointing to the faucet and the knob, we say there is much, much more to the story. And so, as you explain to us that you have aggressors who live upon your Earth who would like to take from you everything that you have, we say to you that they cannot. Unless you invite them through your thought, aggressors will not be part of your experience. That is *Law*, in your physical setting or in our Non-Physical setting.

Is There Value in Losing One's Life?

Jerry: Haven't you said that through having these life experiences, that's how we learn our lessons? But when a person loses their physical life in the process of some violent experience, have they learned any lesson?

Abraham: It is not that you are being offered "lessons." We do not like that word very much, for that sounds as if there is some order of that which you should, or must, learn, and there is none of that. It is that your life experience brings you knowing, and you become wiser and broader through that knowing.

What must be understood before you can appreciate the value, even in the loss, of physical life, is that you are adding unto a greater, broader experience than the one you know as your collective experience here in this physical body. Everything that you are now living adds unto that broader knowing. And so, even when you are removed from your focus through this body, all that you have experienced here will be part of that greater knowing that you hold. And so, yes, there is even value in having an experience that removes you from this physical body. It is not for nothing.

I Am the Culmination of Many Lifetimes

Jerry: Are you saying that losing my life is an experience that somehow adds to all of the experience of that broader Being?

Abraham: It is, indeed. You have lost your physical life on many occasions. You have lived thousands of lifetimes. That is the reason why your zest for life is so great. We could not express to you in words the number of lifetimes that you have lived, let alone much detail from each of them; you have had so much experience that memory of all that experience would confuse and hinder you here. And so, as you are born into this body, you come forth not remembering that which has been before because you do not want the distraction of all that memory. You have something much better than that: You have an *Inner Being* that is the culmination of all of those lifetimes of experience.

Just as now you are that which you are as a culmination of all that you have lived, there is little value for you to sit here and talk about the things you did when you were 3 or 10 or 12. Of course, you are that which you now are *because* of all of that . . . but to continue to look back into your past and regurgitate those experiences does not add much unto that which you now are.

And so, as you accept that you are this magnificent, highly evolved Being, and as you are sensitive to the way you feel, then you have the benefit of your *Emotional Guidance System*—as to the appropriateness of anything that you are about to do—based upon the way you feel.

You are physical Beings, and you are knowing you, the physical you, while most of you are not knowing yourself from your broader perspective. The physical you is a magnificent and important you, but it is also an extension of a broader, greater, wiser, certainly older, you. And that *Inner You* made the decision to come forth to be focused in this body because it wanted the experience of this lifetime to add unto the knowing of the greater, broader *Inner You.*

Why Don't I Remember My Past Lives?

It was agreed, before you came, that you would not have memory—muddling, confusing, hindering memory—of all that you have lived before, but that you would have a sense, a *Guidance,* that comes forth from within. And it was agreed that the *Guidance* would be in the form of emotion, which would be manifested to you in the form of feeling. Your *Inner Being* cannot respond in thought at the same time that you are transmitting a thought, and so, your *Inner Being* has agreed to offer you a *feeling* so that you can know the appropriateness of what you are feeling, speaking, or doing in the context of your greater or broader intentions.

Every time you set forth a conscious intention of something you want, your *Inner Being* factors all of that in. And so, as you are more *deliberate* in that which you offer, in the form of *intent:* "I want, I intend, I expect," your *Inner Being* is able to factor all of that in to give you clearer, more specific, more appropriate *Guidance.*

Many physical Beings, because they do not understand that they are the creator of their own experience, do not set forth deliberate intentions. They resign themselves to taking what comes, not understanding that they are the *attractor* of what comes. But under those conditions, it is more difficult to *allow,* because you feel that you are a victim. You feel that you are vulnerable; you feel that you are not in control of what comes, so you feel you must guard yourself from what may come, not understanding that you are the inviter of what comes. That is why we say that *an understanding of how you are getting what you are getting is essential before you will be in a position of being willing to allow yourself, or to allow any other.*

child abuse?
rape?

What about When Sexuality Becomes a Violent Experience?

Jerry: Another area that I've felt some discomfort with would be morality relating to sexual practices. I've now reached the point of allowing others to have their sexual choices, but I still feel uncomfortable when someone uses force against another person in *any* area. Is there a point, again, that I can get to so that whatever they do, whether one uses force or not, it won't affect my thinking?

Abraham: No matter what the subject is, it is important to understand that there are no victims. There are only co-creators.

You are all, as magnets, attracting unto you the subject of your thought. And so, if there is one who gives much thought to, or one who speaks much about, rape, then it is very likely that they will be the "victim," by their words, of such an experience. Because, by *Law,* *you attract unto you the essence of that which you give thought to.*

As you give *thought,* feeling emotion, you launch your creation, and then as you *expect,* it is your experience. And so, there are many who launch creations that they do not actually receive in their experience because they only do half of the equation. They launch it by giving thought, even emotional thought, but then they do not *expect,* and so they do not receive. This is true of the things you *do* want, as well as the things that you *do not* want.

What Is My *Expectancy* Around This Issue?

We've offered the example of going to the horror movie where you are stimulated to much clear, vivid thought through the sound and picture that is coming forth from the movie. Now you have launched the creation of this scenario as you have given thought, usually with great emotion, but as you leave the theater, you say, "It was only a movie; that would not happen to me." And so, you do not complete the *expectancy* part.

Notice, in your society, that the more that is offered regarding any topic, the greater the public *expectancy* of it. In the same way the greater the *expectancy* of the individuals, the greater the likelihood is that they will attract it.

Do not give thought to those things that you do not want, and you will not have them in your experience. Do not speak of that which you do not want, and you will not attract it into your experience. And so, when you understand that, then, as one who is observing others having experiences that they do not want, you are not so filled with negative emotion, because you understand that they are now in the process of receiving an understanding of how all things come to them.

Now, true, none of us feel joy in watching another being raped or watching another being robbed or murdered. Those are not pleasant experiences. But when you come to the point of understanding how you attract these events into your experience, you will no longer give thought to that—*and then you will no longer be one who is even <u>seeing</u> any of that.*

You draw into your experience that which you give thought to. Your television confuses it, because you turn on your television, intending to have entertainment, and then newscasters bring to you those sudden news bulletins where you are told of some horrible event happening. But when it is your intent to see—no matter what you are doing—only that which you want to see . . . you will be drawn away from the television before such a bulletin is offered.

I Am Prepaving My Future Right Now

When you see something in a newspaper or magazine that begins to bring forth a little negative emotion, you can immediately set it aside rather than continuing with it and receiving more negative emotion as the *Law of Attraction* is adding to the subject. But even beyond that, in this moment, as you are intending to attract unto you only that which you want, you will begin prepaving so that your future action will not need to be so definite. You will not be drawn to the television. You will not be drawn to the newspapers. Instead, you will be drawn, by the *Law of Attraction,* to the subject of your deliberate intent.

The reason so many of you are drawn to subjects of indeliberate intent is because you do not have deliberate intent. You are not saying often enough what you *do* want, and so you are attracting *some* of all of it. The more deliberate you are in what you want, the more pre-paving you will be doing, so that less action will be needed to get unwanted things out of your experience. You will not be ambushed by your television, so to speak, or ambushed by the predators of your society—for the Universe will have prepaved something different for you.

But What about the Innocent Little Child?

Jerry: Many people will accept your basic premise about creating through thought, Abraham, but the point where I see a number of people stub their toe, so to speak, or find difficulty with your teachings is when thinking about innocent children. They'll ask, "But what about the little children? How could little children have thoughts that would bring them physical deformities, ill health, or a violent invasion of their bodies of some sort?"

Abraham: It is because the babies have been surrounded by those who are having those thoughts, and so they have been receiving (the essence of) those thoughts.

Jerry: Something like telepathy?

Abraham: That is correct. You see, long before the child is speaking, the child is thinking. But you cannot know how clear in thought that little child is, because he has not yet learned to verbally communicate with you. He is not yet communicating his thoughts.

Jerry: The child is not thinking in *words*. That is, I can sense that a child is having thoughts long before he or she is speaking words.

Abraham: The child *is* thinking, and receiving vibrational thought from you on the day that he enters your environment. That is the reason why beliefs are transmitted so easily from parent to child, from parent to child, from parent to child. The child is vibrationally receiving your fears and your beliefs, even without your spoken word. *If you want to do that which is of greatest value for your child, give thought only to that which you want, and your child will receive only those wanted thoughts.*

Shouldn't Others Fulfill Their Agreements with Me?

Jerry: Abraham, regarding *Allowing,* I still have, creeping into my mind, an old saying: *One has a right to swing their arms as much as they want* (which to me was "Allowing"), *as long as they don't interfere with my right to swing my arms, or as long as they don't hit my nose.*

In other words, as I go through life and I'm allowing other people to be, do, and have whatever they want, if that interferes with something we have previously agreed to in business, sometimes it's a little difficult not to, at least, call for a sticking to our agreement or to the fulfilling of their responsibilities as we had previously agreed.

Abraham: As long as you have concern that another can interfere in your experience, or that another can swing his arms into your face, then you do not yet really understand how it is that you get what you get. You can begin, today, to think only of what you want; and then begin, today, to attract only what you want. Your question comes forth because yesterday, or somewhere in your past, you did not understand this, and you were inviting—through your thought—those who swing their arms into your face. And so, now, in this moment, you ask, "What do I do about it?"

If there are those in your experience who are swinging their arms in an uncomfortable way, take your attention from them and they will go away, and in their place will come those who feel comfortable to you, who are in harmony with you. But what usually happens is, as they swing their arms, as they do the things you do not want them to do, you give your attention to that. You get angrier about it, you get more upset about it, and by the *Law of Attraction,* you attract more of the essence of that, until soon you have more than one in your experience. There are two, or three, or many. . . . Take your attention from that which does *not* please you, put your attention upon that which *does* please you, and you will then change the momentum. Not instantly, but it will begin to change.

If, every morning for the next 30 days, you begin your day by saying: *I intend to see; I want to see; I expect to see, no matter who I am working with, no matter who I am talking with, no matter where I am, no matter what I am doing . . . I intend to see that which I want to see,* you will change the momentum of your life experience. And all things that now displease you will be gone from your experience and will be replaced by things that *do* please you. It is absolute. It is *Law.*

I Will Never Get It Wrong . . . or Done

When we say that from your Non-Physical Perspective, from the perspective of that which you were even before you became focused in this physical body, that it was your intent to become an *Allower* and to understand the *Art of Allowing*—it is so. *What we want you to understand is that you never get it completed. You are not like a table that is imagined, then created, and then is finished. You are continually in the state of becoming. You are in the process of growth, eternally. But you are always that which you are in this moment.*

You want to understand the *Laws of the Universe* so well that you become at one with them. You want to understand how it is that things come to you so that you do not feel like a victim, or vulnerable to the whims of others swinging their arms.

It is hard for you to understand these things when you are in the middle of what seems to be two worlds: the world that you created before you understood these things that we have talked about here, and the world that you are in the process of creating now that you are understanding more clearly. And so, some of the things that are in your experience because of the prepaving or the prethinking of your past do not fit very well with what you *now* want. And so, we know there is a little bit of discomfort as you are in this transitional stage, but there will be less and less and less discomfort as you are clearer and clearer and clearer about what you want. Much of the clutter of past momentum is now moving from your experience.

When you are in the state of positive emotion and considering only what *you* are doing or thinking or speaking, you are *Allowing yourself*. When you are in the state of positive emotion regarding your view into *another's* experience, you are *Allowing another*. It is that simple. . . . And so, you cannot have negative emotion about yourself and be in the state of *Allowing* yourself.

To be an *Allower* is to be one who feels positive emotion, which means that you must control what you are giving your attention to. It does not mean that you get everything in your world whipped into shape so that everything and everyone is just the way you want it to be. It means that you are able to see, and therefore solicit forth, from the Universe, from your world, and from your friends, that which is in harmony with you, while you let the other parts go unnoticed by you—therefore unattracted by you, and therefore not invited by you. That is *Allowing*, you see.

And we will tell you, friends, *Allowing* is the most glorious state of Being you will ever achieve on a long, ongoing basis. For once you are an *Allower*, you are spiraling upward and upward, for there is no negative emotion to balance you out and bring you down. There is no backward swing of the pendulum. You are forever and gloriously moving forward and upward!

৩৩৩ ৡৡৡ

PART V

Segment Intending

The Magical Process of *Segment Intending*

Jerry: Abraham, my feeling is that the combination of the ingredients of the *Law of Attraction,* the *Science of Deliberate Creation,* and the *Art of Allowing* . . . and then added to that, this next one, the *Segment Intending Process,* seems to comprise the total recipe for making things happen in general. Would you speak to us about the *Segment Intending Process.*

Abraham: Once you understand that you are the creator of your experience, then you will want to identify more clearly what you desire so that you may allow it into your experience. Because until you have stopped to identify what you really want, there is not a possibility of *Deliberate Creation.*

You do not want the same thing in every segment of your life experience. In fact, in every day, there are many segments that carry many different intentions. And so, the point of this *Segment Intending* essay is to help you understand the value of stopping many times during your day to identify what it is you want most so that you may add emphasis, and therefore power, unto that.

There is very little that you are actually living in this day that is a result of only what you are thinking in this day. But whenever you are stopping, segment by segment, and identifying what it is you want in this segment, you are setting forth thoughts that begin to prepave your future experience whenever you are entering segments that are similar.

In other words, let us say that you are getting into your vehicle and you are alone, so intending communication with someone else, or clarity of listening to what another is saying, is not a very important intention. But intending safety and smooth-flowing traffic, and arriving refreshed and on time are intentions that are very well placed in this segment as you are traversing from one place to another. The identification of your *intention* as you are entering this segment of driving not only affects *this* segment, but it sets forth a prepaving into your future so that at future times when you are getting into your vehicle, you will have, in fact, prepaved or created circumstances and events that will be to your liking.

It is possible that, in the beginning, even though you are identifying, segment by segment, what you want, there will still be some momentum from past thoughts that you have set forth. But in time, as you are setting forth, segment by segment, what you want, you will have prepaved a path before you that is very much to your liking. And then you will not have to take so much action in the moment to get things to be the way you want them.

I Can *Segment-Intend* My Success

Technically, all of your creative power is in this moment. But you are projecting it not only into this moment, but also into the future that exists for you. And so, the more you are willing to stop and identify what you want in *this* segment, then the greater, clearer, and more magnificent your future path will be. And each of your moments will be better and better and better, also.

The purpose of this essay is to offer, to those who want it, a practical process with which to put into immediate practice the primary *Laws of the Universe*, in order to give you absolute and deliberate control of your life experience. And while to some, this may seem to be a very broad overstatement, for it seems to most that you cannot control the experiences of your life, we want you to know that you can.

We have come forth to assist those of you who are here, now focused in physical bodies, to understand specifically how you attract everything you are attracting—and to assist you in understanding that nothing comes to you unless you invite it through your thought. And that once *you* begin looking into *your* life experience and begin to see the absolute correlation between what *you* are speaking, what *you* are thinking, and what *you* are getting, then you will clearly understand that, indeed, you are the inviter, you are the attractor, and you are the creator of your physical experience.

These Times Are the Best of Times

You are living in a wonderful time, in a highly technologically advanced society where you have access to stimulation of thought from all around your world. Your access to that information is of great benefit, for it provides you with the opportunity for expansion, but it can also be a source of immense confusion.

Your ability to focus upon a narrower subject brings forth more clarity, while your ability to focus upon many things at once more often brings confusion. You are receptive Beings; your thought processes are very fast, and as you are considering only one subject, you have the ability, by the power of the *Law of Attraction*, to bring forth more and more clarity upon that subject until you can literally accomplish anything regarding it. But because of the availability in your society of so much stimulation of thought, very few of you remain focused upon any one subject long enough to take it forward very far. Most of you find yourselves so distracted that you do not have an opportunity to develop any one thought to any great degree.

The Purpose and Value of *Segment Intending*

And so, *Segment Intending* is the process of deliberate identifica-tion of what is specifically wanted for this moment in time. It is done with the intent of bringing forth from all of the confusion of what is considered to be your total life experience, your aware-ness of what you most want in this particular moment. And as you take a moment to identify what that *intention* is, you bring forth tremendous power from the Universe, and all of it is funneled into this very specific moment in which you now stand.

Think of your thoughts as magnetic. (Indeed, everything within your Universe is magnetic, drawn unto that which is like unto itself.) And so, whenever you are contemplating or focusing upon even a small negative thought, by the power of the *Law of Attrac-tion*—it will grow larger. If you are feeling particularly disappointed or sad, you will find yourself attracting others who are not feeling much different, for the way you *feel* is your *point of attraction*. And so, if you are *unhappy,* you will attract more of that which makes you unhappy. Whereas if you *feel good*, you will attract more that you consider to be good.

Since you attract or invite into your experiences the others with whom you interact; the people who surround you in traffic; the people you rendezvous with while shopping; the people you meet while you're walking; the subjects that people discuss with you; the way you are treated by your waiter at the restaurant; the waiter assigned to you at the restaurant; the money that flows into your experience; the way your physical body looks and feels; the people you date (this list could go on to include everything in your experience)—it is of value to understand the power of your *now* moment in time. The point of the *Segment Intending Process* is to clearly direct your thought to those things that you want to experi-ence by identifying the elements of life that are most important to you in this particular segment of your life.

When we say to you that *you are the creator of your experience,* and *there is nothing in your experience that you have not invited,* some-times we are met with resistance. The resistance comes because many of you have things in your life that you do not want. And so, you say, "Abraham, I would not have created this thing that I do not want." We agree, you would not have done it on purpose, but we will not agree that you have not done it. For it is through your thought—and only through and by *your* thought—that you are getting the things that you are getting. But until you are ready to accept that you are the creator of your experience, then there is not much that will be offered here that will be of value to you.

The *Law of Attraction* affects you, whether you are consciously aware of it or not; and *Segment Intending* will help you be more aware of the power of your thoughts because the more you deliberately apply it, the more the details of your life will reflect your *Deliberate Intent.*

Your Society Offers Much Stimulation of Thought

You live in a society that offers much stimulation of thought, and as you are open and receptive to that, you may very well be attracting more thoughts, and thereby more circumstances and events and people than you have the time or desire to deal with.

In just one hour of your exposure to your media, there is tremendous stimulation that is offered to you, and it is not a wonder that you often find yourself absolutely overwhelmed and that many of you have shut down completely, closed to all things, because there is so much coming to you so fast.

This *Segment Intending Process* will offer you the solution, for as you are reading the words that are offered here, your confusion will be replaced with absolute clarity; your feeling of being out of control will be replaced by a feeling of being in control; and for many of you, a feeling of stagnation will be replaced with a glorious, invigorating feeling of fast-forward motion.

Confusion comes forth when you are considering too many things at one time, while clarity comes forth while you are more singular in thought—and it all hinges upon the Law of Attraction. As you set forth a thought regarding any subject, the *Law of Attraction* immediately goes to work to deliver more stimulation of thought regarding that subject. As you are moving from thought to thought to thought to thought, the *Law of Attraction* is offering you more thought regarding the thought, the thought, and the thought. And that is the reason you often find yourself feeling overwhelmed, for by the *Law of Attraction,* you have now summoned information upon a great many subjects.

In many cases, that information will come forth from your past; in many cases, it will come forth from those who are closest to you, but the end result is all the same: You are considering so many things that you are moving forward in no one specific direction—and the result, of course, is a feeling of frustration or confusion.

From Confusion to Clarity to *Deliberate Creation*

As you choose any one primary subject that you want to ponder, the *Law,* the *Universe,* will deliver unto you more regarding that specific thought. But instead of many thoughts coming from many directions—even conflicting, opposing directions—the thoughts and the events that *now* come forth will all be in harmony with the primary thought that you have set forth. And thus, there will be a feeling of clarity, and even more important than the feeling of clarity will be the understanding that you are moving forward in your creation. *When you consider many subjects at the same time, you generally do not move forward strongly toward any of them, for your focus and your power is diffused, whereas if you are focusing upon that which is most important in any point in time, you move forward more powerfully toward that.*

Dividing My Days into *Segments of Intentions*

The point at which you now stand, the point from which you are now consciously perceiving—that point is a *segment.* Your day may be divided into many segments, and there are not two of you who would have precisely the same segments. On one day your segments may be different from the next, and all of that is fine. It is not necessary to have a rigid schedule of segments. It *is* important that you identify when you are moving from one segment, and therefore from one set of intentions—into another.

For example, when you wake up in the morning—you are now entering a new segment. That time that you are awake before you get out of bed—that is a segment. . . . That time that you are preparing yourself for your next activity—that is a segment. . . . When you get into your vehicle—that is another segment, and so on.

Whenever you realize that you are moving into a new segment of life experience, if you will pause for a moment and set forth aloud, or in your own mind, what you most want as you are moving into that segment, you will begin, by the powerful *Law of Attraction*, to solicit thoughts, circumstances, events, and even conversation or action from others that will harmonize with your intent.

As you take the time to recognize that you are moving into a new segment and you go even further by identifying what your dominant intentions are within it, you will avoid the confusion of being swept up by the influence of others or even the confusion of being carried by your own less than deliberate habit of thought.

I Operate and Create on Many Levels

In every segment of your life experience, you are operating on many levels. There are those things that you are *doing* in the segment. (Doing is powerful creating.) There are those things that you are *speaking* about in the segment. (Speaking is powerful creating.) And there are those things that you are *thinking* in the segment. (Thinking is powerful creating.) Also, within each segment, you may be considering what is happening in your *present;* you may be considering what has already happened in your *past;* or you may be considering what is about to happen in your *future.*

When you are thinking about what you want in your future, you begin attracting the essence of that which you want for your future. But because your present has not yet been prepared for it, it will not likely come into your present—but it will begin its motion forward. And as you are moving forward toward that future place, so are those events and circumstances to which you have given thought.

The Thoughts I Think Today Are Prepaving My Future

Here is the process that we refer to as *Prepaving:* In your present, you give thought to your future so that when you get to that future time, your future has been *prepaved,* or prepared, for you by you. And so, much that you are experiencing today is as a result of your thoughts about today that you thought yesterday and the day before and the year before and the year before. . . .

Every thought that you think that is directed <u>toward what you want</u> for your future is of great benefit to you. Every thought that you are thinking about your future that <u>you do not want</u> is a disadvantage to you.

As you think of vitality and health—and want it and expect it in your future—you are prepaving and preparing that for yourself. But as you fear or worry about decline or disease, you are also preparing or prepaving *that* for your future.

Segment Intending will assist you whether you are in your *now,* thinking about your *now;* or are in your *now,* thinking about your future. For, in each of these cases, you will now be deliberate in your creating. And that is the point of the *Segment Intending Process.* Whether you are specifically intending something to do or say in this moment, or whether you are prepaving your future in this moment, it is of great value for you to do it on purpose.

When you get into your vehicle, if you will set forth your deliberate intent for safety on this journey, you will literally attract the circumstances that will bring that about. Now, of course, if you had intended that as you were beginning many previous journeys . . . if, in your past, as you viewed your future, you had wanted and expected safety, then those intentions set forth in advance would have already begun to prepave your future, and your *Segment Intending* would now be adding unto that intent . . . strengthening it, indeed.

I Can Prepave Life or Live by Default

If you have not prepaved and you are not deliberately intending in this segment, then you are living life by default, and so, the possibility of being swept up in the confusion or intentions of someone else is likely.

Two Beings who are in two separate vehicles, arriving at the same point at the same time and experiencing a collision . . . are two Beings who have not intended safety. They were living life by default, and they now find themselves, in their confusion, attracting one another, you see.

If you want and expect to receive the subject of your intent, it will be. But if you do not take the time to establish what you want, then you are attracting, by the influence of others or by the influence of your own old habits, all sorts of things that you may or may not want. We agree that there are some things that you attract accidentally or by default that you *do* like, just as there are some things that you attract, not intentionally, but by default, that you do *not* want, but there is not much satisfaction in attracting by default. The true joy of life is in *Deliberate Creation.*

PAUSE DURING DAY TO SAY !
As I Am Feeling, I Am Attracting

Now, this is the key to your *Deliberate Creating:* See yourself as this magnet, attracting unto you the way you *feel* at any point in time. When you *feel* clear and in control, you will attract circumstances of clarity. When you *feel* happy, you will attract circumstances of happiness. When you *feel* healthy, you will attract circumstances of health. When you *feel* prosperous, you will attract circumstances of prosperity. When you *feel* loved, you will attract circumstances of love. *Literally, the way you feel is your point of attraction.* And so, the value of *Segment Intending* here is that you pause many times during your day to say, *This is what I want from this segment of my life experience. I want it and I expect it.* And as you set forth those powerful words, you become what we call a *Selective Sifter,* and you will attract into your experience what you want.

You see, the Universe—indeed, the very world in which you live—is filled with all sorts of things. There are things that you like very much, just as there are things that you do not like very much. But all of that comes into your experience only by your invitation through thought. And so, if you are taking the time, many times in a day, to identify what you want, and setting forth your statement of desire and expectation, you will gain the magnetic control of your own experience. No more will you be the "victim" (there is not really such a thing), and no more will you be the indeliberate attractor or the default attractor. Once you begin to segment your day, to identify many times in the day what it is you do want, now you are a *Deliberate Attractor*. And that is a joyful experience.

What Is It That I Now Want?

The reason that *Segment Intending* is so effective is because there are so many subjects you could consider, but when you try to do so all at the same time, you become overwhelmed and confused. The value of intending, segment by segment, is that as you focus more precisely on the fewer details of this moment, you allow the *Law of Attraction* to more powerfully respond; and you are less likely to confuse the issue further with your contradictory thoughts of doubt, worry, or an awareness of lack.

For example, when your telephone rings, you might pick it up and say, "Good morning." And when you hear who it is, you say, "Hello, there, hold just a second please," and then you say to yourself, *What is it that I most want to achieve in this conversation? I want to uplift the other person. I want to be understood. I want the other person to understand me, and I want the other to be positively influenced in the direction of my desire. I want the other to be stimulated and excited by my words. Indeed, I want this to be a successful conversation.* Then, when you come back on the line, you have *prepaved*. And now, that other one will respond to you much more in accordance with your desire than if you had not taken that time.

When another person has initiated the telephone call, they know what *they* want. And so, you must take a moment to identify what *you* want. Otherwise, by the power of their influence, they may achieve what they want—but you may not.

If you want many things all at the same time, it adds confusion. But when you focus upon the most important *specifics* of what you want in any particular moment, you bring about clarity, power, and speed. And that is the point of the *Segment Intending Process:* to stop as you are entering a new segment and to identify what it is you most want so that you may give it your attention and, therefore, draw power unto that.

Some of you are focused during some segments of your day's experience, but there are very few of you who are focused during very much of your day. And so, for most of you, an identification of segments, and an intent to identify what is most important within those segments, will put you in the position of being a deliberate magnetic attractor, or creator, in each of your segments through-out your day. And not only will you now find that you are more productive, but you will find that you are happier. For as you are deliberately intending, and then allowing and receiving, you will find great contentment.

You are growth-seeking Beings, and as you are moving forward, you are at your happiest; while, when you have that feeling of stagnation, you are not at your happiest.

An Example of a Day of *Segment Intending*

Here is an example of a day in which you are not only aware of each new segment that you are moving into, but you are also setting forth your intentions for each segment.

Let us say that you are beginning this process at the end of this day before you go to sleep. Recognize that entering into the sleep state will be a new segment of life experience. And so, as you are lying there with your head on the pillow, getting ready to go to sleep, set forth your intention for that time: *It is my intention for my body to completely relax. It is my intention to awaken rested, refreshed, and eager to begin my day.*

sleep

The next morning as you open your eyes, recognize that you have now entered into a new segment of life experience, and that the time you remain in bed until the time you remove yourself from the bed is a segment. Set forth your intent for that time: *While I'm lying here in my bed, I'm intending to have a clear picture of this day. I'm intending to become exhilarated and excited about this day.* And then, as you are lying there in the bed, you will feel that refreshment and that exuberance for the day coming upon you.

As you get out of bed, you have entered into another new segment of life experience. This may be the segment in which you are preparing yourself for the day. And so, as you are entering the segment of brushing your teeth and taking your bath, let your intent be: *I intend to acknowledge my wonderful body and to feel appreciation for the magnificent way it functions. I intend to be efficient in my grooming and to bring myself to looking my best.*

As you are preparing your breakfast, let your intent for this segment be: *I will select and prepare this wonderful, nutritious food efficiently. I will relax and eat it in joy, allowing my wonderful body to digest and process it perfectly. I will choose the food that is best for my physical body at this point in time. I will be replenished and refreshed by this food.* And as you set forth this intention, you will notice that as you are eating, you are feeling yourself more rejuvenated, replenished, and refreshed. And you will enjoy the food more than if you had not set forth that intent to do so.

As you get into your automobile and are traveling to your destination, let your intent in this segment be to travel from one place to another in safety, to feel invigorated and happy as you are moving forth, and to be aware of what the other drivers are intending or not intending so that you may move through traffic in a state of flow—safe and efficient.

When you get out of your automobile, you have now entered into a new segment. And so, pause for a moment and imagine yourself walking from where you are to where you intend to go. See yourself feeling good as you walk; intend that you will move efficiently and safely from point to point. Intend to breathe deeply as you feel the vitality of your body, and intend to feel the clarity of your thinking mechanism. . . . Set forth your vision or your intention for the next segment you are about to enter. Imagine your greeting of the staff or of the employer. . . . See yourself as one who uplifts others, having a smile ready. Recognize that everyone you meet is not deliberate in their intending, but know that by your deliberate intending, you will be in control of your life experience; and you will not be swept up by their confusion, or by their intent or influence.

As you are moving through a day of Segment Intending, you will feel the power and the momentum of your intentions building, and you will find yourself feeling gloriously invincible. And as you are seeing yourself again and again in creative control of your own life experience, you will feel as if there is nothing that you cannot be, do, or have.

For *Segment Intending,* Carry a Small Notebook

Of course, your segments will not be just as we have offered, and they will not be the same from day to day. In only a few days, you will find it very easy to identify each new segment and to identify what you most want from it, until very soon you will be able to clearly expect good results from every segment of your day.

Some of you may find it more efficient and effective to carry a small notebook and to physically stop to identify the segment while you write a list of your intentions in your notebook. Since writing something down onto paper is your strongest point of focus, in the beginning of your application of this *Segment Intending Process* you may find your notebook to be of great value.

You have gathered some questions for us upon this topic of *Segment Intending?*

Isn't There Some Goal to Be Achieved?

Jerry: Abraham, to me, *Segment Intending* appears to be the ideal vehicle for an instant practical application (and realization) of the *Law of Attraction,* the *Science of Deliberate Creation,* and the *Art of Allowing.* In other words, by immediately coupling our now-conscious awareness of these *Laws* (which your teachings have clarified for us) with this *Segment Intending Process,* we can each immediately discover for ourselves how our thoughts can affect our manifestations.

I have been equating *Segment Intending* with the equivalent of intending a series of small goals (or intentions) of which we can, almost instantly and consciously, experience their manifestations. This brings me to my next question: Is there not a basic overall goal (or intention) for us to complete in this physical life?

Abraham: There is. And just as *Segment Intending* is the intent that is closest to this moment in which you are now living, your intent as you emerged into physical expression is on the other end of that, so to speak. In other words, here you are now, intending what you most want from this moment, yet this moment is being affected by thoughts you have had about this moment even before your birth into this physical body. As you emerged into this physical body from that inner, broader perspective, you did have intentions, indeed, but your intentions from this physical conscious perspective are dominant now.

You are not a puppet acting out that which has been intended before. You have the choice, in every moment, to decide what is most appropriate from your ever-evolving perspective, *for you have grown beyond that which you were as you emerged into this body—for this life experience has already added unto that perspective.*

Can the Goal of Happiness Be Important Enough?

Jerry: So, since I don't consciously know what these specific, individual, overall goals are, would there be anything more important than having a goal to just be happy?

Abraham: You have hit upon the way to know what it is you have intended as you have come forth from your inner perspective. In other words, you said, "Since I don't consciously know what these specific, individual, overall goals are." The reason you do not consciously know what the specific goals are is because there were no specific goals. *You had, before your physical birth, general intentions, such as being happy, being an uplifter, having continuing growth . . . but the specific processes or vehicles through which you will achieve any of those things is up to you to decide here and now. In this time, you are the creator.*

How Can We Recognize That We're Having Growth?

Jerry: Let's take the intention that you mentioned: *growth.* How can we recognize when we're having growth?

Abraham: Since you are a growth-seeking Being, you will have positive emotion whenever you are recognizing your growth, and you will have negative emotion whenever you are feeling stagnation. You see, you do not necessarily have conscious recognition of the thoughts or intentions of your inner or broader perspective—but you do have communication. *All physical Beings have communication from their Inner Being in the form of emotion, and so, whenever your emotion is positive, you can know that you are in harmony with your inner intentions.*

What's a Valid Measure of Our Success?

Jerry: Then, what do you see, Abraham, from your Non-Physical perspective, as a valid measure of our being successful at what we're doing here?

Abraham: You have many ways of measuring your success. In your society, your dollars are a measure of success; your trophies are a measure of success—but from our perspective, the existence within you of positive emotion is your greatest measure of success.

Can *Segment Intending* Speed Up Our Manifestations?

Jerry: So, this process of *Segment Intending* can not only speed up our getting whatever we want, but then it can also make this experience that we're having more pleasurable, and more within our conscious control (and therefore more successful). Is that what it's about?

Abraham: It is absolutely "more within your conscious control" as you are consciously setting forth your intentions. The alternative is to not make a decision about what you want, and therefore, in your confusion, to attract a little bit of everything; and, in attracting a little bit of everything, there is some that you like and some that you do not like. The point of the *Segment Intending Process* is that you will always be attracting that which you deliberately want. No more creating by default; no more attracting what you do not want.

You are right when you say that it can speed up the process, for it is your clarity that speeds. Of course, you are physically creating as you move piles of dirt from one place to another (or whatever it is you are doing), but you have not accessed the power of the Universe unless your thoughts have brought forth emotion. When emotion is present—whether it is positive or negative—you have now accessed the power of the Universe.

When you really, really want something, it comes to you very fast. When you really, really do not want something, it comes to you very fast. The idea of Segment Intending *is to set forth your thought of what you want, focusing upon it clearly enough, in this moment, that you bring forth emotion about it. Your clarity brings the speed.*

Meditations, Workshops, and the *Segment Intending* Processes

Jerry: Let me clarify some terminology with you, please. There are three different Processes. One you call *Segment Intending*. One you call having a *Workshop*. And the other one you speak of sometimes, in terms of other people's words, is *Meditation*. Would you clarify what the differences and purposes of these three processes are?

Abraham: Each of these processes is for a different intention. And so, your question fits in perfectly with our subject of *Segment Intending,* for as you are about to enter into any of these three processes, it is a good idea to know *why* you are entering into them, and what you *expect* to receive.

A time of *Meditation,* by your terms, is a segment in which you are intending to quiet your conscious thinking mechanism in order to sense the *Inner World.* It is a time of physical distraction, or detachment from the physical, so that you may sense that which goes beyond the physical. There are different reasons for this detachment, and it is important that, as you are entering this segment, you identify what your reason is. Your reason in this segment of *Meditation* may be that you simply want a detachment from the world that is confusing or troubling you. You want some time of refreshment. When *we* encourage *Meditation,* it is with the intent of allowing the opening of your passageway so that you may blend the *Inner You* that exists in the *Inner Dimension* with the conscious physical you that is here in this physical body. *Meditation is a withdrawing of your focus from the physical conscious world, and an allowing of your focus to align with the Inner World.*

Now, the *Workshop Process* is a segment where you are intending to give specific and precise thought to the details of what you want, and to bring forth, by the *Law of Attraction,* clarity. In other words, you want to ponder your desire so specifically that you bring forth the power of the Universe to speed your creation. The *Workshop* is the time in which you guide your thoughts in the direction of your specific desire, aligning your thoughts, in this moment, with the desires that your life has helped you identify. *In your physical world, you cannot have a physical experience until you have created it first in thought. And so, the Workshop is that place where you give deliberate thought to, and where you begin the deliberate attraction of, the thing, or things, that you want.*

The process of Segment Intending is to simply recognize that you are moving into a segment where what you are intending is different from the last, and then to stop and identify what you are now wanting. Segment Intending is the process by which you eliminate the predominant hindrances to your Deliberate Creation: influence of others who may have different intentions than you do, or the influence of your own old habits.

How Can I Consciously Begin Feeling Happy?

Jerry: I've heard you suggest that we get to the point of feeling happy before we begin intending something. Would you give us some different ways of consciously generating the feeling of joy, or of bringing forth the feeling of positive emotion?

Abraham: Before we do that, we want to point out the great value in your being happy. You are like magnets, and the way you *feel* is your *point of attraction.* And so, if you are feeling unhappy, if you are giving thought to that which you do not want (which is what would be bringing forth the *feeling* of unhappiness), then you are attracting more of what you do not want. *There is great value in being happy, because only from the point of being happy can you attract that which you want, but it is also your most natural state of being. If you are not allowing yourself to be happy, you are holding yourself away from who-you-really-are.*

As you notice that you are, in this moment, happy, take the time to identify what things are present that may be affecting your happiness. For many of you it can be listening to music that is in harmony with you in the moment. For some it will be petting their cat or taking a walk or making love—or playing with a child. For some it will be reading a passage in a book. For some it will be calling a friend who is uplifting. There are many ways of doing it.

It is of value to find many touchstones to use to uplift yourself so that you may always use another approach to bring forth that feeling of happiness. *Take notice of that which uplifts you and remember it, and then, when you specifically want to feel uplifted, use that as a touchstone to your happiness.*

But What about When Those Around Me Are Unhappy?

Jerry: You have said that we can be happy under almost all conditions. But how can that be accomplished when we are observing someone who is experiencing extremely negative conditions?

Abraham: *You can be happy only under the condition of giving thought to what you want. And so, you can be happy under all conditions if you are clear enough and strong enough in your wanting to give your attention only to what you want.*

Jerry: But what if there are those you feel obligated to occasionally be with who do or say things that make you feel very uncomfortable, and yet you still want to try to please them because you feel guilty whenever you don't do or be what they want? How would you suggest we be happy in a situation like that?

Abraham: It is true. It is more difficult to remain happy or positive when surrounded by others who are unhappy, or when you are surrounded by or involved with those who want something different from you than you want to give them. But what we have noticed as we have been interacting with physical Beings is that while you may have an experience that only lasts five or ten minutes, and while that experience may be unpleasant and uncomfortable, the majority of your negative emotion comes forth not *during* the minutes of that negative experience, but they come forth in all the hours that you ponder and chew upon it *after* the experience. *Usually, there is much more of your time spent in thought of the negative thing that has happened than in the actuality of what is happening.*

The majority of your negative emotion could be eliminated if, in those times when you are alone, you would focus upon what you now want to think about. And then, in those briefer encounters, in those smaller parts of your life experience where you are actually being harassed by another, you will grow stronger in your ability to not notice the harassment so much and, in time, the *Law of Attraction* will not bring you to those experiences because those thoughts will no longer be active within you.

Can I *Segment-Intend* Around Unplanned Interruptions?

Jerry: So, let's take a situation in which people truly want to have a feeling of an orderly progression forward, but their intentions are quite often diverted by what I call *unplanned interruptions*. What sort of *Segment Intention* would you suggest in a situation like that?

Abraham: Of course, as your *Segment Intending* becomes more defined, and as you get better at it, you will automatically have far fewer interruptions. You have been encouraging the interruptions because of your lack of *Segment Intending* in the past.

As you begin your day envisioning free-flowing, smooth-flowing life experiences, you will have eliminated some of those interruptions already. And, for those interruptions that do come forth, you can deal with those segment by segment, simply by saying at the beginning of the interruption, *This will be brief, and I will not lose my train of thought. I will not lose the momentum that I have set forth. I will deal with this quickly and efficiently, and I will get on with what I was doing.*

Could *Segment Intending* Expand My Usable Time?

Jerry: I've said throughout the years, *I wish that there was a lot more of me so I could experience all of the wonderful things that I want to experience.* Is there a way that we can use *Segment Intending* so we can experience more experiences—that is, so we can do more of the things we want to do?

Abraham: You will find, as you become efficient with your *Segment Intending*, that you will have many more hours in your day to do those things you want to do.

Many of the things that you want have not been coming forth to you because you have not given clarity of thought to them and attracted them. And so, the *Segment Intending* itself will give you that which you are seeking in this question. *By being clear about what you want and no longer contradicting it with opposing thoughts, you will* *enable the <u>Laws of the Universe</u> to do their work, and you will not feel a need to offer so much action to compensate for inappropriate thought. By offering deliberate thought, you will harness the power of the Universe, and it will require far less time for you to accomplish much, much more.*

Why Isn't Everyone Creating Life on Purpose?

Jerry: Since we each have the choice of creating what we really want—on purpose—or creating by default and receiving indiscriminately both the wanted and the unwanted, then why does it seem like the majority of people choose by default?

Abraham: Most are creating their experiences by default because they do not understand the *Laws;* they really do not understand that they have those choices. They have come to believe in fate or luck. They say, "This is reality; this is just the way it is." They do not understand that they have control of their experience through their thought. It is like playing a game where they do not know the rules, and soon they grow tired of the game because they believe that they have no control over it.

It is of great value for you to give your conscious attention to what you specifically want, otherwise you can be swept up by the influence of that which surrounds you. You are bombarded by the stimulation of thought. And so, unless you <u>are</u> setting forth the thought that is important to you, you can be stimulated by <u>another's</u> thought that may or may not be important to you.

If you do not know what you want, then it is good for you to set forth the intent: *I want to know what I want.* And as you set forth that desire, you will begin attracting data; you will begin attracting opportunity; you will begin attracting many things to select from—and from the steady parade of ideas that will flow to you, you will get a better idea of what you specifically desire.

Because of the *Law of Attraction,* it is easier to just observe things as they are than it is to choose a different thought. And as people observe things as they are, the *Law of Attraction* brings them more of the same, and in time, people come to believe that they do not have control.

Many are taught that they are not allowed to choose, that they are not worthy of choice, or that they are not capable of knowing what is appropriate for them to choose. In time, and with practice, you will come to understand that you can tell, by the way you are feeling, the appropriateness of your choice, for when you choose the direction of thought that agrees with your broader perspective, your joy is your confirmation of the appropriateness of your thought.

How Important to Our Experience Is *Wanting?*

Jerry: Now the person who doesn't even say, "I want to know what I want," but just says, "As far as I know, I don't want anything," or "I've been taught that it is wrong to have desire," and is in some kind of a flat, listless state, would you have anything to say to this person?

Abraham: *Is the desire to have no desire—in order to achieve a greater state of worthiness—not also a desire? Wanting is the beginning of all Deliberate Creating. And so, if you refuse to allow yourself to want, then you are really refusing the deliberate control of your life experience.*

You are physical Beings, indeed, but you have a Life Force; an Energy Force; a God Force, a Creative Energy Force, that flows into you from the Inner Dimension. Your doctors, in all of their notice of it, do not know much about it. They know that some have it and some do not. They will say, "This one is dead; he has no Life Force." *Creative Life Force flows into you for the extension outward toward whatever you are giving your attention. In other words, it is the process by which your thought brings to you whatever desire you are giving thought to.*

The more you give thought to that which you desire, the more the *Law of Attraction* sets those things into motion, and you can feel the momentum of your thoughts. When you do not think about what you desire, or when you think about what you want and then immediately think about the lack of it, you hinder the natural momentum of thought.

That "flat, listless state" you are describing is caused by your constant slowing of the momentum of thought with your contradictory statements.

Why Do Most Settle for So Little?

Jerry: Abraham, we live in a nation where almost everyone is able to eat every day, and has a place to live and has clothing. Almost everyone at least gets by in some way. I meet people who say, "You know, I have enough to get by, but somehow I can't build up my desires strong enough to bring anything major or special into my life." What would you say to a person in that situation?

Abraham: It is not that you do not desire more, but you have somehow convinced yourself that you cannot *have* more. And so, you want to avoid the disappointment of wanting something and not getting it. It is not because you do not want it that you are not receiving what you want—it is because you are focusing upon the *lack* of it. And, by the *Law of Attraction,* you are attracting the subject of your thought (the lack of it).

Whenever you want something and then you say, *"But* I have wanted it and I did not get it," now your attention is upon the lack of what you want, and so, by *Law,* you are attracting the lack. Whenever you are thinking about what you want, you are feeling exhilarated, you are feeling excited, and you are feeling positive emotion; but as you are thinking about the lack of what you want, you are feeling negative emotion; you are feeling disappointment. The disappointment that you are feeling is your *Emotional Guidance System* saying to you, "What you're giving thought to is not what you want." And so, we would say, allow yourself to want a little, put your thought upon what you want, feel the positive emotion that comes forth from wanting, and let the disappointment go away. And, in your giving thought to what you want, you will attract it.

Speak to Us about *Prioritizing Our Intentions*

Jerry: You've given Esther and me a process that we've had great results with, and I'd like it if you would elaborate a little bit on it. It is the process you refer to as *Prioritizing Our Intentions.*

Abraham: Although you do not hold all of your intentions at any one point in time, you often have many intentions that do all relate to this point in time. For example, you are interacting with your mate, you want clear communication, you want to uplift yourself, you want to uplift your mate . . . and you may want to influence your mate to want the same. In other words, you want harmony.

It is important for you to identify which intentions you want most to fulfill, because as you <u>prioritize</u>, you give your singular attention to what is most important; and as you give it your singular attention—you attract power unto the intention that is most important to you.

So, let us say that you have begun your day, but you have not clearly identified your segments. You have blundered into the day, as most do, moving from one thing to another, buffeted about by the impulses and desires of others, or by your old habits. The telephone is ringing, your children are asking for this and that; your mate is asking you questions, and you find yourself not clear about anything, but you are moving about in a day that, for most, is rather normal.

Now, you find yourself involved in a discussion where you have not taken the time to identify what you want, and, let us say, you find yourself in a disagreement with either your children or your mate or with anyone—it matters not who it is. You feel "warning bells" coming forth from your *Inner Being.* The negative emotion is mounting in you for a number of reasons: You are a little bit mad at yourself for getting into this muddle because you have not intended clearly, but even beyond that, you are upset because you are in disagreement with what the other person is intending, what the other is stating, or what the other is wanting.

If you catch yourself in that segment and you say, *What do I most want right now in this situation?* you may recognize that *feeling harmony* really is your dominant intent—getting along with your wife or your child or whatever. That is, having a harmonious relationship is far more important than this insignificant issue. And as you recognize that harmony is what you want most, suddenly you are clear; your negative emotion goes away, and you make a statement such as, *Wait, let's talk. I don't want to argue, for you are my*

(handwritten margin note: harmony as priority*)*

best friend. I want us to have harmony. I want us to be happy together. And as you make that statement, you will disarm the other. You will remind the other that that is the dominant intent of him or her, also. And now, from your new and focused *prioritized intention,* which is harmony, you may take a fresh view of this less important subject at hand.

Here we will give you a statement that, if you will set it forth at the beginning of all segments of your life experience, will serve you very well: *As I'm entering this segment of life experience, it is my intent to see that which I want to see.* And what that will do—when you are interacting with others—it will help you to see that you want harmony; that you want to uplift them; that you want to put across your idea effectively, and that you want to stimulate their desire to one that harmonizes with your desire. That statement will serve you very well.

How Detailed Must My Creative Intentions Be?

Jerry: As we intend forward motion, how detailed should we be in the ways or the means, and how specific should we be in the outcome or the manifestations, of our intentions?

Abraham: You want to be detailed enough in your thought of what you want that you bring forth positive emotion about it, but not so detailed that the thought of what you want brings forth negative emotion. As you vaguely intend something, your thought will not be specific enough—and therefore not powerful enough—to bring forth the power of the Universe. But on the other hand, you can become too specific before you have collected enough data to support your belief. In other words, as you become specific, but it challenges your beliefs about the subject, you may find yourself feeling negative emotion. *And so, become specific enough in your intentions that you bring forth positive emotion, but not so specific that you bring forth negative emotion.*

Must I Regularly Repeat My *Segment Intentions?*

Jerry: Abraham, let's speak more in terms of *Segment Intending*. Since it would be very tedious to give our attention to every small detail involved in every moment, could we not just intend safety, say, the first thing in the morning? And then wouldn't that keep us safe for the rest of the day?

Abraham: It is not necessary that you intend it again and again and again, although there is value in reiterating what is most important to you at any point in time. *Once you have set forth your intent for safety and you begin feeling safe, now you are at the point of always attracting safety. At any time that you may feel unsafe, that is the time, again, to set forth your reinforcement of safety.*

Could This *Segment Intending Process* Hinder My Spontaneous Reactions?

Jerry: Could *Segment Intending* hinder our spontaneity, or our ability to react to a situation in the moment, in any way?

Abraham: *Segment Intending* would hinder your ability to react by *default*—but it would strengthen your ability to react *deliberately*. Spontaneity is wonderful as long as you are spontaneously attracting what you want. It is not so wonderful when you are spontaneously attracting that which you do not want. We would not replace deliberate creating with spontaneous-creation-by-default, at any cost.

The Delicate Balance Between Belief and Desire

Jerry: Abraham, would you take a moment here and speak to us about what you have called *the delicate balance of creating—between wanting and believing?*

Abraham: The two sides in this balance of creation are *want it* and *allow it.* You could also say *want it* and *expect it.* You could also say *think about it* and *expect it.*

The best scenario is to desire something and to bring yourself into the belief or expectation of achieving it. That is creation at its best. If you have a slight desire for something and you believe you can achieve it, the balance is complete and it becomes yours. If you have a strong desire for something but you doubt your ability to achieve it, it cannot come, at least not right now, for you must bring your thought of desire and your thought of belief into alignment.

Maybe you have been stimulated to a thought of something that you do not desire, but because you have often heard reports of this thing happening to others, you believe in the possibility of it. So your slight thought of this unwanted thing and your belief in its possibility make you a candidate for the achievement of that experience.

The more you think of what you want, the more the *Law of Attraction* will bring the evidence of it to you, until you *will* believe it. And when you understand the *Law of Attraction* (and it is easy to come to know it because it is always consistent) and you begin to deliberately direct your thoughts, your belief in your ability to be, do, or have anything will come into place.

When Does *Segment Intending* Lead to Work?

Jerry: We are physical Beings, and we're taught to believe that in order to get a financial return, our hard work is important. But you don't mention much about the physical action. How does *hard work* or *physical action* fit into your creative equation?

Abraham: The more attention you give to an idea through thought, the more the *Law of Attraction* responds—and the more powerful the thought becomes. By prepaving, *Segment Intending,* and imagining in your *Creative Workshop,* you will then begin to feel inspiration to act. *Action that comes from the feeling of inspiration is action that will produce good results, for you are allowing the Laws* *of the Universe to carry you.* If you take action without deliberately prepaving, though, often your action feels like hard work because you are attempting to make more happen in this moment than your action alone can accomplish.

If you will think your creation into being and then follow through with inspired action, you will find your future ready and waiting for you to arrive, and then you can offer your action in order to enjoy the fruit of your true creative power instead of incorrectly trying to use your action to create.

Which Is the Best Choice of Action?

Jerry: So, when there are a lot of different actions that we *could* be taking in order to accomplish something specific, how can we finally decide, in the last moment, which of these different possible actions would be the most effective for us to use?

choices

Abraham: By imagining yourself taking the potential act, and then noting how you feel while you are imagining that action. If you have two choices, envision yourself taking one choice and note how you feel about it. And then envision yourself taking the other choice and see how you feel about that. The way you feel about the potential action will not be clear to you, however, unless you have taken the time to first identify your intentions and put them in an order of priority. And once you have done that, then making the decision of what is the most appropriate action will be a very simple process. You will be using your *Emotional Guidance System.*

How Long Should I Wait for the Manifestation?

Jerry: Let's say there are those who are waiting for something to manifest right now and they find themselves getting a little discouraged because what they've been intending isn't there yet. How long should they wait before there are any visible signs of success? And what would be some signs that it *is* going to happen?

Abraham: As you have set forth your intent to have something and you are looking expectantly for it, it is now on its way to you, and you will begin to see many signs of it: You will see others who have achieved something like it, which will stimulate your wanting; you will take more notice of aspects of it in many different directions; you will find yourself thinking about it and feeling excited about it often; and you will be feeling very good about that which you want—those will be some of the signs that what you want is on the way.

When you understand that the majority of your creative effort is spent in defining what you want and then aligning your thoughts to that desire, you may then realize that the majority of the creative process is taking place on a vibrational level. Therefore, your creation can be nearly complete, as much as 99 percent complete, before you see physical evidence of it.

If you will remember that the positive emotion you are feeling in anticipation of your creation is also evidence of its progress, then you will be able to move steadily and quickly toward the outcomes you desire.

Can I Use *Segment Intending* to Co-create?

Jerry: Abraham, how can we use this *Segment Intending Process* in order to mutually accomplish a goal with another person?

Abraham: The better the job you have done in your own *Segment Intending,* the more powerful your thoughts will be about *your* desire—and then your power of influence will be stronger. And so, as you interact with others, it will be easier for them to catch the spirit of your idea.

It is also extremely helpful for you to use the *Segment Intending Process* to evoke the best from others. If you expect them to be unhelpful or unfocused, you will attract that from them; while if you expect them to be brilliant and helpful, you will attract *that* from them. If you have spent some time bringing your thoughts to a powerful place before your physical meeting, you will have a much more satisfying co-creation for yourself, and for them.

How Can I Convey My Intent More Precisely?

Jerry: I recall, throughout the past years, that quite often I would go into a situation that I felt was very important, but the other person and I would talk back and forth, and then after I left, I would think, *Gee, I could have said* and *I should have said* and *I wanted to say,* but I didn't. So instead of feeling a sense of accomplishment when the interaction was over, I often felt a sense of frustration. How could I have avoided that?

Abraham: By thinking about your desired outcome *before* you enter into the conversation, you will get a momentum going that will help you more clearly convey your meaning. It is also of value to recognize that in this combining of thoughts, ideas, and experiences, together you have the potential of creating something even greater than you could create on your own. So prepaving your positive expectation of their contribution will put you in a position of rendezvousing with their clarity, power, and value. In this good-feeling alignment, your mind will be clear, you will evoke clarity from the other, and, together, you will have a wonderful co-creation.

Jerry: What if a person doesn't want to upset others, or hurt their feelings, or anger them when the subject of the interaction might be a controversial thing? In other words, if you're interacting with someone who has some *conflicting* desires, and yet you can see there could be some mutually *beneficial* goals that could be achieved if a potential controversy could be avoided, how can a situation like that work out for all persons involved?

Abraham: By intending—as you are moving into the segment—to focus upon those things that you *do* have in common; to focus upon your points of harmony; to give very little attention to what you are *not* agreeing upon, and to give your great attention to the things you *do* agree upon. That is the resolution in all relationships. *The trouble with most relationships is that you pick out the one little thing that you do not like and then give that most of your* *attention. And then, by the <u>Law of Attraction,</u> you solicit more of what you do not want.*

Can One Have Prosperity Without Working for It?

Jerry: You've told us many times that we can have it *all*. Let's take a situation where people want prosperity, but they don't want to go to work or find a job. How would you suggest they bridge that quandary?

Abraham: By considering the intentions separately. If they want prosperity, but it is their belief that prosperity comes only through working, then they will not be able to have prosperity because they do not want to do the only thing that they believe will bring it forth. But as they consider prosperity, singularly, then by not coupling it with the work that they are resisting, they will be able to attract prosperity.

You have come upon something very important; it is what we call conflicting intentions, or conflicting beliefs. *The solution is simply a matter of taking your eye off of what is conflicting, and putting it upon the essence of what you want.*

If you want prosperity and you believe that it requires hard work and you are willing to offer the hard work, there is no contradiction, and you will achieve a level of prosperity.

If you want prosperity and you believe that it requires hard work and you are averse to hard work, there is a contradiction in your thinking, and you will not only have a difficult time offering the action, but any action you offer will not be productive.

If you want prosperity and you believe that you deserve it, and you expect it to come to you just because you want it to, there is no contradiction in your thinking—and the prosperity will flow. . . . Pay attention to how you are feeling as you are offering your thoughts so you can sort out the contradictory thoughts, and as you eliminate the contradictions regarding anything that you desire, it must come to you. The *Law of Attraction* must bring it.

When the Job Offers Rained, They Poured!

Jerry: So let's say that there's a person who hasn't been able to find a job after months and months of wanting and trying, and then as soon as they *do* receive a job that they want, four or five other good offers come in all at once, say, in that same week. What would be the cause of that?

Abraham: The reason why the job was so long in coming was because, rather than focusing upon what they *wanted,* which was the job, they were focusing upon the *lack* of the job—pushing it away. Once they broke through and received a job, then the focus was no longer on the *lack* of it—*the focus was on what was wanted, so now, they began receiving more of what had been prepaved.* In your example, the desire grew stronger even though the belief was weak, so in time, the *Law of Attraction* yielded what this person was feeling the strongest. They tortured themselves unnecessarily, however, by not taking the time to clean up their thoughts.

Why Are Adoptions Often Followed by Pregnancies?

Jerry: Is that why if a couple who hasn't been able to get pregnant for years adopts a child, then, suddenly, the wife often becomes pregnant?

Abraham: It is the same story, indeed.

Where Does Competition Fit into the Intentions Picture?

Jerry: Another question: How does *competition* fit into the picture?

Abraham: From our perspective, in this vast Universe in which we are all creating, there truly is no *competition,* for there is enough abundance on all subjects to satisfy all of us. You put yourselves in a

competition

position of competition by saying that there is only one prize. And that can bring forth a little discomfort, for you want to win; you do not want to lose, but often the attention is upon losing rather than on winning.

When you put yourself in the position of competition, the one who wins is always the one who is clearest about his wanting, and most expectant of it. It is Law. If there is any value in competition, it is this: It stimulates desire.

Would Strengthening My Willpower Be an Advantage?

Jerry: Is there any way people could strengthen their will so that they could get more of what they want and less of what they don't want?

Abraham: Utilizing the process of *Segment Intending* certainly could accomplish that. But it is not so much "a strengthening of the will" as it is thinking thoughts that the *Law of Attraction* then adds to. *Willpower* can mean "determination." And *determination* can mean "deliberately thinking." But all of that sounds like harder work than is really required. *Simply give thought to what is preferred, consistently throughout the day, and the Law of Attraction will take care of everything else.*

Why Do Most Beings Stop Experiencing Growth?

Jerry: It seems to me that most people in our society, by the time they've reached the age of 25 to 35, have gone about as far as they're going to go as far as their development and growth. They have the home they're going to have; the lifestyle they're going to have; the job they're going to have; the beliefs, politics, and religious convictions they're going to have; and even the variety of personal experiences that most of them are going to have. Do you have any idea what the cause of that is?

Abraham: It is not so much that they have had *all* of the experiences that they are going to have, it is that they are no longer attracting *new* experiences. In the new experience, there is excitement and more desire, but many of them are no longer deliberately setting forth their desire; they are more or less resigned to *what-is*.

Giving attention to *what-is* only attracts more of *what-is*. While giving attention to what is wanted attracts change. And so, there is a sort of complacency that comes about, simply because the *Laws* are not understood.

Most people stop deliberately reaching for expansion because they have not understood the *Laws of the Universe*, and so, they have been unintentionally offering contradictory thoughts resulting in not getting what they want. When your belief of what you can accomplish contradicts your desire of what you would like to accomplish, even hard work does not yield good results, and over time you just get tired.

Coming into conscious awareness of the *Laws of the Universe* and then beginning to gently guide your own thoughts to that which you prefer will begin to produce positive results immediately.

Jerry: So, let's say that a person has reached a particular point in life where they find themselves in what I would call a downward or negative spiral. How could they use *Segment Intending* to start that spiral moving back up again?

Abraham: Your *now* is powerful. In fact, all of your power is right here, right now. So if you will focus upon where you are right now and stop to think about what you most want from this segment only, you will find clarity. *You cannot, right now, sort out everything that you want about every subject, but you can, right now, define what you prefer from here. And as you do that, segment after segment, you will find a newfound clarity—and your downward spiral will turn upward.*

How Do We Avoid Influence from Old Beliefs and Habits?

Jerry: Abraham, it seems to be particularly difficult for most of us to discard our old ideas, beliefs, and habits. Would you be willing to give us an affirmation that would assist us in avoiding any influence from our past experiences and beliefs?

Abraham: *I am powerful in my now.* We are not encouraging a discarding of old ideas, for in trying to get rid of them you actually only think about them more. And, some of your old ideas are worth keeping. Just be more aware of how you are directing your thoughts, and make a decision that you want to feel good. *Today, no matter where I am going, no matter what I am doing, it is my dominant intent to see that which I want to see. Nothing is more important than that I feel good.*

Jerry: So, if people are witnessing the negatives being broadcast through the media, or even listening to the problems that they might hear presented by their friends, how could they keep that negativity from offsetting them?

Abraham: By setting forth the intent, in every segment of their life experience, to see that which they want to see. And then, even from the most negative presentations, they could see something that they do *want*.

Is It Ever Okay to State What Isn't Wanted?

Jerry: Is it *ever* okay for us to state the things we *don't* want?

Abraham: Stating what you do not want can sometimes bring you to a clearer picture of what you *do* want. But it is good to quickly get off the subject of what you do *not* want, and onto the subject of what you *do* want.

Is There Any Value in Researching
Our Negative Thoughts?

Jerry: Abraham, do you ever see any value in trying to identify the specific thought that may have brought forth some negative emotion?

Abraham: There can be value in it for this reason: *What is most important when you recognize that you are thinking a negative thought is to, in whatever way you can, stop thinking the negative thought.* If there is a belief within you that is very powerful, then you may find that this negative thought will come up again and again and again. And so, you continually have to divert your thought from that negative thought onto something else. In that case, it is of value to recognize the troublesome thought and modify it by applying a new perspective to it. In other words, mold the conflicting belief into one that is not so conflicting—and then it will not keep coming up and haunting you.

What about When Others Don't
Consider My Desires Realistic?

Jerry: If there's someone who knows what we want to accomplish (and it's something really far beyond the average), and this person tells us that our desires are "not realistic," how can we avoid being influenced by that?

Abraham: You can avoid others' influence by having given thought, even before your interaction with them, to what is important to you. *Segment Intending* will be of great value here. *As others insist that you look at "reality," they are influencing you to be rooted to this spot like a tree. As long as you are seeing only what-is, you cannot grow beyond it. You must be allowed to see what you want to see if you will ever attract what you want to see. Attention to what-is only creates more of what-is.*

How Is It Possible to "Have It All in 60 Days"?

Jerry: You've essentially said, that within 60 days, we could have everything be the way we want it to be in our lives. How would you suggest that we go about doing that?

Abraham: First, you must recognize that everything that you are now living is a result of the thoughts that have been offered by you in the past. Those thoughts have literally invited, or set up, the circumstances that you are now living. And so, today, as you begin setting forth your thought of your future and seeing yourself as you want to be, you begin the alignment of *those* future events and circumstances that will please you.

As you give thought to your future—your future that may be 10 years; your future that may be 5 years; or your future that may be 60 days away—you literally begin prepaving. And then, as you move into those prepaved moments, and as that future becomes your present, you fine-tune it by saying, *This is what I now want.* And all of those thoughts that you have put forth about your future, right down to this moment when you are now intending what action you want to take, will all fit together to bring you precisely that which you now want to live.

And so, it is a simple process of recognizing day by day that there are many segments. And as you are entering into a new segment, you need to stop and identify what is most important to you so that by the *Law of Attraction,* you may attract that unto you for your consideration. The more thought you give to something, the clearer you become; the clearer you become, the more positive emotion you feel and the more power you attract. And so, this business of *Segment Intending* is the key to swift and *Deliberate Creation.*

We have enjoyed interacting with you very much on this most important subject. There is great love here for you.

Now You Understand

Now that you understand the *rules,* so to speak, of this marvelous game of *Eternal Life* that you are playing, you are now destined to have a wonderful experience, for now you are in creative control of your own physical experience.

Now that you understand the powerful *Law of Attraction,* you will no longer misunderstand how it is that things are happening to you or to any other you may be observing. And as you practice and become proficient at directing your own thoughts toward those things that you desire, your understanding of the *Science of Deliberate Creation* will take you anywhere you decide to go.

Segment by segment, you will prepave your life experience, sending powerful thoughts into your future to make it ready for your joyful arrival. And by paying attention to the way you feel, you will learn to guide your thoughts into alignment with your *Inner Being* and who-you-really-are as you become the *Allower* you were born to be—destined to a life of fulfillment and never-ending joy.

We have enjoyed this interaction immensely.

And, for now, we are complete.

— **Abraham**

Index

expansion of, 82
experience and, 164
power of, 179
thoughts and, 57
unlimited, 43, 44, 112
unplanned interruptions, *Segment Intending Process* and, 174
unrealistic, 112
unwanted, the, 30, 47–48, 54–55, 66, 68–69, 84, 93, 98, 108, 110, 115, 121–22, 127–28, 132, 135, 146, 148
    attention to, 137
    hiding from, avoiding, 59
    ignoring, 133
    speaking of, 147
    thought(s) and, 147
unwanted people, hiding from, avoiding, 59
unworthy, 34
uplift, 66, 103, 109, 127–28, 131, 167, 179
uplifter, 169
uplifting oneself, 172
uplifting the world, clear decisions and, 130–31
upset, 150, 178
upward spiral, 111, 151
usable time, 171
usable time, *Segment Intending Process* and, 174–75

value, 41, 47, 95–96, 143, 149, 158, 172, 175, 190
variety, 38, 55
vehicle, 42, 123
vibrate, 68
vibrational, 182
    nature, 76
    thought, 149
    Universe, 37
vibrationally similar, 83
vibration(s), 16, 30–31, 32, 34–35, 37–38, 47, 65, 92–93, 95–96, 103, 127
    action and, 61–62
    activation of, 33, 54
    alignment with desires, 61, 63, 71, 112
    amplifying, 127
    attraction of opposites and, 61
    Being and, 76
    desires and, 61
    dominant, 61, 63, 66
    essence and, 58
    harmony and, 79, 82–83, 85
    improvement of, 47
    improving, 64
    lacks and, 61

matching, 33, 36–37, 48, 58, 66
offerings of, 56, 65
practicing, 62
signals of, 60–61
thoughts and, 71
victims, 57, 142, 145–46, 150, 164
    attraction and, 58
violating, 141–42
violence, 141, 146, 148
virtue (positive), 101
vision of, 42
visualization, 62, 76, 99–101, 108
    imagination and, 98
vitality, 40, 162
vocation, 98
vulnerability, behavior of others and, 121–22, 145, 150

wait, 182
wake up, 161
walk (taking a), 172
walking, 166
walls, 122
Walsch, Neale Donald, xiii–xv
    Conversations with God, xiii
want/desire, 33, 36–37, 43, 47, 50, 56, 86, 92–94, 99–100, 102, 109–10, 120, 129, 135, 150, 158, 161, 164, 170, 175, 181, 191
wanted, the, 16, 61, 66, 93, 98, 132, 146, 165, 189
    Allowing and, 133
    blended intention(s) and, 57
    evil and, 54–55
    the future and, 137
    knowing, 175
    troubles of others and, 127–28
    victims and, 58–59
wanting, 28, 37, 39, 47, 62, 67, 138, 173
    Allowing balance and, 85–86
    believing balance and, 180–81
    importance of, 176
    knowing what, 55–56
    versus needing, 128–29
    passion and, 93–94
    thoughts of lack and, 56
    thoughts of receiving and, 56
warning bells, 50, 84, 178
warnings, 58
wars, 121
water (moving), 41
wealth, 99, 139
Websites, xviii, 194
"Welcome, little one, to planet Earth," 39
Well-Being, 23–25, 65, 66, 82, 95, 128,

135, 139, 193
    enhancing, 69–70
    focusing on, 127
wellness, 51
well-stocked kitchen, the world as, 63
what-is, 38, 91, 100
    attention to, 190
    focusing on, 188
    growth and, 190
what isn't wanted, 189
who-you-really-are, 63, 68, 79–80, 84, 172
willing, 56, 128, 145
willingness, 44, 138
willpower, *Segment Intending Process* and, 96, 186–87
wins, 112
withdraw attention, 69
within selves, 71, 79, 80
wonderful life, 64
words, 37, 65, 128, 148
    attraction and, 71
    enhancing Well-Being and, 69–70
    as example, 130

    versus examples, 103
Words do not teach, 124
work, 39, 41–42, 104, 181
    prosperity and, 185
work (hard), 56, 99, 102, 104–6
working for, 42, 185
Workshop, Creative, 42, 44, 47, 49, 89, 93, 99, 100, 170
Workshop Process (Creative), 41
worlds, perceivers and, 63, 66, 76, 77, 151
worldwide events, 47
worthiness, 34, 79, 82, 95, 103–4
write reasons, 87
wrong (vs. right), 71, 80, 130–31, 150
wrong actions, others and, 131–32

yawning sensation, 16
you, 72
you are the creator of your experience, 158
your now, 76, 78
    power and, 189

About the Authors

Excited about the clarity and practicality of the translated word from the Beings who call themselves *Abraham*, **Esther** and **Jerry Hicks** began disclosing their amazing Abraham experience to a handful of close business associates in 1986.

Recognizing the practical results being received by themselves and by those persons who were asking meaningful questions regarding finances, bodily conditions, and relationships—and then successfully applying Abraham's answers to their own situations—Esther and Jerry made a deliberate decision to allow the teachings of Abraham to become available to an ever-widening circle of seekers of answers to how to live a better life.

Using their San Antonio, Texas, Conference Center as their base, Esther and Jerry have traveled to approximately 50 cities a year since 1989, presenting interactive *Art of Allowing Workshops* to those leaders who gather to participate in this progressive stream of thought. And although worldwide attention has been given to this philosophy of Well-Being by Leading-Edge thinkers and teachers who have, in turn, incorporated many of Abraham's concepts into their best-selling books, scripts, lectures, and so forth, the primary spread of this material has been from person to person—as individuals begin to discover the value of this form of spiritual practicality in their personal life experiences.

Abraham—a group of obviously evolved Non-Physical teachers—present their broader perspective through Esther Hicks. And as they speak to our level of comprehension through a series of loving, allowing, brilliant, yet comprehensively simple essays in print and in sound—they guide us to a clear connection with our loving *Inner Being,* and to uplifting self-empowerment from our Total Self.

The Hickses have now published more than 700 Abraham-Hicks books, cassettes, CDs, videos, and DVDs . . . and they may be contacted through their extensive interactive Website at: **www.abraham-hicks.com;** or by mail at Abraham-Hicks Publications, P.O. Box 690070, San Antonio, TX 78269.